Getting on the Upside of Hurricanes

Tony Gillen

Disclaimer of Warranty/Limit of Liability

Hurricanes, floods and natural disasters in general are not predictable events. As a result, neither the publisher nor author are able to accept any responsibility or liability if any particular action, tip or strategy does not work for anyone in any particular situation, and so any perceived or implied liabilities or warranties are specifically disclaimed without exception or limitation. This work is sold with the understanding that neither the publisher nor author is engaged in rendering legal, professional or technical advice or services concerning natural disasters. Everyone should seek specific advice about specific needs from appropriate, competent specialists and neither the publisher nor author shall be liable for any loss or damage arising from the purchase, reading or implementation of information in this work. The fact that an organization or website is referenced in this work does not mean that the information or organization is endorsed by the publisher or author. Readers should be aware that websites may have changed or disappeared between when this work was written and when it is read.

The author and the publisher have taken all reasonable care to ensure that all material in this work is original, or is in the Public Domain, or is used with the permission of the original copyright owner. However, if any person believes that material for which they own the copyright has found its way into this work without permission, they should contact the author, via the publisher, who will seek to investigate and remedy any inadvertent infringement.

Getting on the Upside of Hurricanes
© Tony Gillen 2009

The right of Tony Gillen to be identified as the author of this work has been asserted by him in accordance with the Copyright, Designs and Patents Act 1988.

All rights reserved. No part of this publication may be reproduced, stored in a retrieval system or transmitted in any form or by any means, electronic, mechanical, photocopying, recording, scanning, or otherwise, except as permitted under Sections 107 or 108 of the 1976 United States Copyright Act, without the prior written permission of either publisher or author other than by a reviewer, who may quote brief passages in a review.

Published by Blue Ocean Publishing
St John's Innovation Centre
Cambridge CB4 0WS
United Kingdom
www.blueoceanpublishing.biz

Typesetting by Norman Brownsword, Spitfire Design
Cover design by David McDougall, McDougall Graphics and Design

A catalogue record for this book is available from the British Library.
ISBN 978-0-9556430-3-3

Acknowledgements

I'd like to begin by thanking Carol and Laura for encouraging me all the way through the summer of 2004 and while I wrote this book. A big thank you is also due to all the professionals and volunteers who worked so hard for so long through that summer. Many of them had their own damaged homes to deal with and many came from other areas, leaving their own families so they could be here helping us.

As part of the story I have mentioned a number of people, including friends and neighbors. I'm grateful to each one of them, not just for all they did but also for giving me the opportunity to say "thank you" to them by way of mentioning them in these pages.

I appreciate the fact that Mr. Wayne Sallade Director of Charlotte County Emergency Management, Mr. Wayne Simons, Ms Lois Thome, Mr. Jim McLaughlin and Mr. Jim Farrell of WINK Television, Dr Steve Lyons of The Weather Channel, Mr. Robert Van Winkle of NBC-2, Mr. Michael Fish of the BBC and to Clear Channel Radio, who either personally or through their companies gave permission for me to use their names.

I am also grateful to FEMA for allowing me to reprint photographs of events from their archives. These are used in the e-book available on-line at www.UpsideOfHurricanes.com

I'm indebted to all the authors of so many guides on preparation for, and recovery from, hurricanes and floods. I have studied those guides extensively both in previous years and as part of my own research for this book. The guides were a foundation for me to build on.

And finally, I'm very grateful to you. You have paid me the great compliment of getting a copy of "Upside". I truly hope you enjoy it. Follow the actions, strategies and tips, feel inspired and empowered. Then go for it. Good luck, God speed and let's all come out triumphant!

Contents

Why you should read this and why I had to write it	1
Charley, Frances, Ivan and Jeanne	3
The Upside Effect	89
Be prepared! – Think ahead, plan ahead	100
Things to do a long time before you are threatened	104
Ready, get set, save	112
Your emergency supplies kit	116
People with special needs	122
Caring for your pets	124
Evacuating safely and successfully	126
During the storm and after the storm	129
Protecting your boat	138
Flooding is definitely worse	140
Afterword	148
Appendix	149

Why you should read this and why I had to write it

There are three main reasons for you to read it:
- **It's a great story!** You'll laugh, you'll cry and you'll come out feeling triumphant. You'll connect or reconnect with 2004 in a lot of very good ways
- **It will inspire you and it will empower you!** It doesn't matter whether you expect a hurricane or a flood. If you intend to do your best for yourself and your family this book will lift you, guide you, direct you
- **You will save money!** Exactly how much depends on how many of the ideas, tips and strategies you use. At very least you'll save many times the cost of this book and, at most, you'll save yourself thousands of dollars.

This book is the most complete list of actions you can take to prepare for storms, floods and other disasters. **"Prepare well, be safe, save money"**!

I have spoken with a lot of people about the summer of 2004; people who got hit in their pocket books and hit in their hearts. And many people, like me, learned that all the preparation they did just wasn't good enough. We did the "obvious" things and most of us did them as the storms were approaching.

This book will help you change your thinking a little to help you save a lot – a lot of effort, emotion, stress, time and money – hundreds or thousands of dollars worth of money. I hope those reasons are enough to make reading this book worthwhile!

Why did I have to write it? I started writing it for myself – to make me feel better, to cleanse my spirit and to lift myself. That was how it started but it soon became much more than that. It became something for everyone else; something to remind us all of the good things – the *Upside of Hurricanes* – something to help change the bad memories and most of all it became something to change what we do in the future.

The more I got into the writing, the more I realized I was trying to create something that would lift others. I wanted to do more than "write a story" or "create a better list of things to do". What I was really trying to do is to take people "out of themselves" by seeing disaster through the eyes of someone else – in this case, me. By doing this, I wanted it to enable people to remember or experience those events of 2004 in good ways. I also wanted to find a way of helping to bring families and neighbors together before a storm hits, so they will be stronger after it hits. And I wanted to put together a list of actions, thoughts, tips, ideas and strategies that included everything, so "might'ves", "could'ves" and "should'ves" just wouldn't exist.

I believe it's important to know that you've done your best. So if you read this, I know you will be "ready" as quickly, as easily and as cheaply as possible – and that'll make you feel good.

No matter what the impending natural disaster you're expecting, I truly believe this book will give you the best and most complete set of actions you'll find in one place.

The last few years have seen some devastating natural events – hurricanes, tornadoes, floods, wildfires. All are different but all have a similar effect on families and friends, neighbors and neighborhoods. I wrote this little book because I wanted to make an important contribution to help everyone be successful – emotionally, practically and financially.

I hope that you close the last page, put the book down and then say to yourself "I know I'm ready, I know my family is ready, we've got this thing *down*. We're *Up* for it!"

And that's a huge upside!

Charley, Frances, Ivan and Jeanne

A quiet day out of the office

Shall I get myself another beer, or shall I get Carol to get me another beer?
Got it! I'll ask Carol to put The Weather Channel on and I'll add 'And while you're at it get me another beer, will you?'
And she'll say 'What's the magic word?'
And I'll say 'Please'.
And she'll get me another beer.
You're brilliant, Tone!

So, after I went and got myself another beer, I switched to The Weather Channel.
That tall, good-looking guy was going on about rain in the mountain states.
'Hello? I don't live up a mountain! I live on the sticky-out bit at the bottom.' And, credit where it's due, they immediately put Dr Steve Lyons on. Now, Dr Steve is one of those good eggs we meet all too infrequently; he articulates well, always wears a long-sleeved white shirt and an appropriate necktie.
'Tell it like it is, Dr Steve,' I said. 'What's going on with Tropical Storm Bonnie?'
Well, it appears that Tropical Storm Bonnie is old news and the world's most respected climatologist has something to say about Hurricane Charley.
Hurricane Charley? Whose idea was it to spell Charley "e-y"?
Not Dr Steve, I'll bet. However, Tropical Storm Bonnie is off into the wild blue yonder and all eyes are on The Gulf.
The Gulf?
My Gulf?

Gulf of Mexico Gulf?

Blood and sand!

Where's Laura? Oh, yes, at work putting all the computers on desks in case it floods in Punta Gorda. I wonder if that's why she went? I wonder if all daughters know things before their fathers do?

So I said to my ever-loving

'Hey, wasn't there a film a few years back called Bonnie and Charley where they both got shot?'

And she said 'No, you're thinking of Butch Cassidy and The Sundance Kid.'

'Oh, yeah, Bolivia.'

I wonder if they get hurricanes in Bolivia. If I'd spent more time listening in my geography lessons, all those years ago, instead of idling my time away on the back row, I'd probably know if Bolivia got hurricanes.

I bet all mountain states get hurricanes.

But at the time there seemed little point in learning about climate. England, where I grew up, doesn't have a climate, it only gets weather. Rather like Florida, actually. Sometimes it rains and sometimes it shines. Sometimes the sun shines and sometimes it rains. The weather men in Florida don't know any more than the weather men in England; they get it right sometimes and they get it wrong sometimes.

And they call it science. And they invent words like "nowcast" and "futurecast" to see if you can keep up. And "daypart forecast". And they like to be called meteorologists, not weather men. I think that's because it makes it all sound so much more scientific. But they still have a hit-and-miss track record.

If mountain states do get hurricanes, would they give them cool names like Hurricane Butch Cassidy? And if they did, and they used up all the alphabet letters too quickly, would they run out of names and have to go alphanumeric? Hurricane A1 doesn't have the same feel, does it? It's not personal.

Anyway, would Lloyds of London let hurricanes be called 'A1'?

Would it cause confusion in insurance circles? Would people go 'Hurricane A1 – that means it's a very good hurricane, no danger there, no sirree, Bob.'?

Or would they go 'Hurricane A1? Good grief that'll make it a top-of-the-list hurricane, best of all possible hurricanes, winds as high as anyone could measure. Whose stupid idea was it to call it A1?'

What if it hit Lloyds?

Could Lloyds claim on their insurance? Would they have to pay anything to anyone else or would everyone else have to pay Lloyds? Unless they were clever, of course, and got the insurance underwritten by Lloyds. "Underwritten at Lloyds" is one of the things people expect when they buy insurance and then Lloyds would have to pay themselves.

What a useless insurance policy that would be.

Imagine it:

"Excuse me we're Lloyds and we've just had a negative encounter with Hurricane A1, can we have some money, please?"

"Yes, write yourself a check out of the insurance pot."

"But it's our pot."

Irony knows no bounds.

Getting in the groove

And Hurricane Charley, according to the good Dr Steve, is heading north.

Quite right.

To Tampa.

That's fair; Tampa never gets much news coverage. Except when the Tampa Bay Bucs won the 30-something Super Bowl. They got coverage then.

"Where are your Buccaneers?"

"On each side of my Buccanhead."

It's an old joke, but it sometimes gets a laugh. Except when you tell it to a Tampa Bay person. Ah well!

'Now, how do you know the hurricane's going to Tampa, Dr Steve?'

Because there's nothing to stop it?

What stops hurricanes?

Cold fronts, that's what. You can't beat a cold front for hurricane-stopping power or at least hurricane-redirecting power.

Where's the nearest cold front?

'Show me the big bendy line with the little triangles on it, Dr S.'

Not there.

No cold front.

Hurricane Charley is definitely going north.

All we'll get is a bit of wind.

And Category 2 isn't all that bad. 115 mph winds. Halve that for every thirty minutes of longitude, or whatever the rule is, and we should just get a strong breeze, just like Hurricane Georges back in 1999. (Hurricane Georges always sounded to me like two or more hurricanes otherwise it would just have been called one George.)

'Well done Dr Steve.'

Enough of weather; I'll see what's on WINK News. Old Jim and Lois usually have something of interest to say.

More Hurricane Charley!

It's going north on WINK, as well. Well, it would, they all copy the same homework. Computer models all say the same thing. I wonder if all computer models are programmed in alphanumeric or do they program everything in color these days?

'Why are you saying it's going north, Jim, and then say it could make landfall anywhere from Naples to Tampa?'

Naples isn't north, Naples is south. What do you mean Fort Myers?

Well, actually Fort Myers is still a way off. Winds up to 100 miles an hour for us if it goes to Fort Myers.

100 miles an hour isn't all that much; I drive at 100 mph sometimes

when I go back to England for a vacation. Only occasionally; I often do about ninety but a hundred isn't much more.

But if this hurricane is going north how can it go to Fort Myers?

To get to Fort Myers it will have to go right. To go right there has to be a cold front in the way. Dr Steve didn't mention the cold front.

What if there's a cold front that Dr Steve doesn't know about?

That doesn't make sense. Dr Steve is in the **National** Hurricane Centre.

National not local.

Dr Steve should know more than Jim and Lois because he's a weather expert.

But just a minute, perhaps Lois and Jim are actually more in the know than Dr Steve. After all, where is the National Hurricane Centre? Could be in Bolivia for all I know. I'm going to stick with Lois and Jim. They're in Fort Myers; they can probably see Hurricane Charley from their desk; or they've got a cameraman at the window looking out to see if he can see anything and then relay up-to-the-second information back to them, so they can look good and sound knowledgeable.

And Jim always wears a suit as well as a tie.

Well, a jacket, anyway. He never stands up so you can't see if it's a proper suit or just a suit jacket. Lois never stands up, either, but she always looks as though she's wearing a very sensible twin set. You can always rely on a news anchor person who wears sensible twin sets.

Hang on! What if they only pretend to wear proper clothes and it's all a sham just for television and just to make me feel I can rely on what they say? What if they don't know?

Of course they know! They're Lois and Jim! And Lois is from Wisconsin.

Go Cheese Heads!

Oh dear, this isn't the relaxing Friday away from the office I was hoping it would be.

Good grief!

Good thing we put up all the hurricane shutters the other day. I only do things like that because the neighbors do and I don't want them to think I'm stand-offish. Actually, we all help each other on our street and we started with Jim and Shirley. That's a different Jim.

This Jim isn't the same as the WINK TV Jim. This is Jim the neighbor and he's just come out of hospital. I've never seen this Jim wear a suit or a suit jacket and he doesn't pretend he knows anything about hurricanes like that other Jim.

So, we put up Jim and Shirley's shutters. Jim did all the technical stuff and Shirley told him what to do. So did Frank. Frank's another neighbor. Frank hasn't got any hurricane shutters but he still wanted to join in and play. Frank doesn't want people to think he's stand-offish, either. Frank has anti-hurricane glass in his windows.

So, while Jim and Shirley were round the front, we were round the back; I put the shutters up in the groove things, Carol put the bolts in and Frank put the nuts on and we said we were a new company called "Hang 'em and Screw 'em". Nobody else thought it was funny, but we did and we kept telling everybody and we would laugh and they would just go "Oh." And then they'd say 'Can you come and help with mine next?' And that's how it went; helping each other to put up shutters. Because that's what we do. We're all that kind of people on our street; someone says let's have a party, so we have a party. Let's go on a trip, so we go on a trip. Let's all drink beer in the middle of the road and call it Oktoberfest. Even neighbors from the next road come to our street parties. It's brilliant living in America.

Anyway, Carol went and helped Joan because her family is on vacation. Which prompted Frank to say,

'Just remembered something; I bought screens for my lanai and I'm not sure how to install them.'

'Not a problem', I replied, 'Carol won't be long, I'm sure she'll be able to . . . ah, you mean me, don't you? Let's go.'

So, off we go to Frank's lanai (which a lot of people spell lania and lani for some reason). It has always fascinated me that some people spell words differently, even simple words like lanai but then we did have a president who didn't know what "is" is.

He goes on television and says "Well it all depends on what you mean by is". Give me a break, Mr. President. Is is is is is not was is is not will be is is is. And that's all there is to it. Politicians!

So we're looking at these screen things. They're like big nets. They're huge. And heavy. It was like he wanted to catch the hurricane or something. There certainly wouldn't be any fish to catch. Fish don't like winds. Or noise, or people splashing about in the water.

That's why when you see someone fishing you shouldn't run up and down the bank and chuck stuff in the water because it frightens the fish and they don't "bite". I didn't think fish bit anyway. I've seen lots of fish in supermarkets and none of them has ever tried to bite me. A couple of fishermen threatened to bite me once, but I think they were more afraid of the stuff I was throwing in the water than the fish were. And I was only eight at the time.

'These are new, aren't they?'

'Yup, we thought they'd be better than huge shutters, but hanging them seems to be awkward.'

'Awkward! I've never seen anything like them. You stand there and take the weight and I'll hang the corner, then we'll move to the next hook.'

Well, we pulled and lifted and tied and sweated and then realized it was upside down.

'Tony, I think it's upside down.'

'It doesn't say which way is "up", so how do you know?'

'It's obvious when you stand back. And that's why it's so difficult; they're meant to go round the other way.'

'Do you think it matters?'

'Yes.'

'Drat.'

So we had the double pleasure of unhooking the thing and re-hooking it and tying down the bottom and then spending the next hour hooking and tying off all the others. I didn't realize their lanai was that big!

Or that I was so unfit.

And then I realized – I'd still not done my front window shutters. I'd forgotten to. This is going to be a long day.

'Hi Dad.'

'Hi Sweetheart. Finished?'

'Yeah.'

'You sound tired. Go in and have a rest; I'll be in soon. Mum's still at Joan's.'

Laura had just returned from putting all the computers and chairs and things at work on desks. She knew that downtown Punta Gorda can flood even in heavy rain storms, so if there's to be a storm surge it will definitely flood. The more electronics you have, and the more wooden things you have, the more you need to get them off the floor – and covered in plastic in case the roof leaks. Technology and fine wooden furniture do not like to stand in water, oh dear me, no.

And I have to say, making enough room in a two car garage for a second car isn't that easy. We leave expensive cars on the driveway and fill the garage with cheap crap – until there's a hurricane on its way, of course, then it's one more thing to go "check" with as you work out how to make enough room for a whole car.

I left my car out because there wasn't enough room for three cars and she is my daughter, so her car must be protected given a choice, especially as mine's older than Lor's. And, anyway, I thought if my car gets hit by a tree or something they might give me a new one. Not that it was going to get hit by a tree because Hurricane Charley is on its way to Tampa (or not, depending on who you listen to).

Earlier I did one of my customer's shutters. They live up north but come down for vacations. Anyway right now they're up north and I like to look after their house while they're away. They've got bimini shutters. I've never done bimini shutters before; they're not much fun but they are very fast. I had to get a screwdriver to help. I'm not very good with screwdrivers.

Ellery, one of our (very witty) neighbors, once said, 'If you want to hide something from Tony, put it behind a screwdriver.' He laughed; I laughed, too, so he would think I thought it was funny.

It was about as funny as a bimini shutter on a stormy day.

And it was really interesting driving around Punta Gorda. Everybody was busy – shutters, shutters, shutters, plywood, plywood, plywood. I bet Home Depot is busy. And Lowe's. And Publix. And Winn-Dixie. And all the other stores.

Everybody buys water and bread in times of feverish hurricane preparation. And beer. They also buy water and bread at Thanksgiving. Have you noticed that?

Do you know why?

I never understood that. At Thanksgiving we all eat lots of turkey and sweet potato and pumpkin pie. We drink wine and beer and soda. But how much bread do you eat? How much water do you drink? I know it's a holiday and the stores close early but, come on, we eat less bread than on any other day of the year, but we all buy extra bread. Doesn't make sense. And it's the same during hurricane preparations. Lots of bread and water – and pizzas. I can understand buying spare batteries – just try getting a battery on a hurricane preparedness day and you'll see what I mean.

Anyway, after you put up all the window shutters and you've secured the garage door and you're still outside, you have to remember that the side garage door is still open and you go in that way.

No, I didn't forget or go into a panic about being stuck outside on my own. I'm just saying so if it happens to you, you can go in through the side door.

Inside it's very dark with all the shutters up, even though it's still daylight. It feels peculiar. And the acoustics change. It just all feels peculiar.

So, after we'd done all the shutters, we thought we'd better do a check thingy, so we checked we'd done everything.

Hurricane shutters. Check.

Extra food. Check.

Bottles of water. Check.

Batteries. Check.

Beer. Check.

Monopoly. Check. I'm not playing Monopoly. Number one the hurricane won't last that long and number two I never win.

Important papers. Not check. Quick, get the important papers from all over the place and put them in one place and then put them in a suitcase and put the suitcase in a plastic bag. Check.

Time for a short rest. Check.

Not such a quiet day after all

Let's check on Jim and Lois again, I'm in need of some reassurance as well as a rest.

Jim and Lois just said 'It's going north' (well that's reassuring) 'and it could make landfall here' (that's not reassuring at all).

And Dr Steve, who knows everything, and therefore has my total admiration and unfailing acceptance of anything he says, is going on about Sanibel and Captiva and Matlacha, but still plays safe and keeps Tampa on the list.

Then I looked at the Doppler Radar real time computer imagery situation at street level as he's talking about "going north".

'Dr Steve, the doughnut bull's-eye thingy just moved a bit to the right! Did you bang the TV with your leg or did that thing just go right a bit? Now come on, Dr Steve, help me out here! Did you just bang that TV monitor with your leg or are you just not looking closely enough at it?'

'What are you a doctor of? **It just went right, a bit!'**

Right means it's closer to me. So if it's heading north and it just went right, that means it's going north-right. And that's where I live. And if the whole hurricane is about an hour from here traveling north-right at 20 miles an hour with an internal wind speed of 115 miles an hour, then it will be here in about an hour. And that's not long enough even to start playing Monopoly.

For crying out loud; it takes longer than an hour to put the cards in order and give out the money and argue about who's going to be banker and if you can buy properties before you go all the way round, or if you have to go round once first and then you buy and I always get the brown one and it's rubbish because everyone who lands on it gets $200 out of the bank first so they never go bankrupt and I spend all my $200 straight away and then go and land on the orange one, or I miss that and land on the green one and that's really expensive and when I get "Chance" I have to pay income tax or school fees or something **and it just went right again.**

I'm going back to Lois and Jim.

'What do you mean it's now Category 4?'

Have you any idea how fast Category 4 is? Category 4 is like 15 miles an hour faster than my roof is supposed to be able to stay on.

'Lois, Jim, Dr S; what are you doing to me? What's happening to my quiet day?'

Still Charley's got a little eye, so he might not see our house especially as it looks like everybody else's all covered in hurricane shutters.

And it still might go to Englewood because it is still going north (a bit).

It's not going north at all, is it?

It's on its way into Charlotte Harbor, isn't it?

The very same Charlotte Harbor which I call paradise and it's a Category 4 hurricane and it's right on my doorstep.

And, come to think of it, the wind is beginning to blow rather loudly and it's gusting even more loudly and we can't see. We have to go to the front garage door because there are little windows in it, but up at the top, so you have to stand on something to see out. They're really just for show, but we had to buy a big thick plastic hurricane shield to go behind it in case of a hurricane, so we are very pleased we got it but it does make it difficult to see out. But we could see enough to see that the wind is really picking up and the trees are waving, bending, twisting. And it's raining.

I'm not feeling relaxed at all.

And I had to come back in just in case the hurricane got me (Carol said) and we all sat and listened to the noise.

It's very disconcerting sitting in a darkened home and hearing loud noises. Why didn't we get some see-through hurricane panels? Why didn't we think harder about all this?

The noise got louder and louder like a very high wind would sound. And the rain lashed against the metal panels and sounded like high speed rain would sound. The gusts are even higher than the regular wind and the noise is even louder and the rain sounds like it's coming out of a high pressure hose. And sometimes it sounds like someone's throwing gravel at the shutters.

The gusts only last for a few seconds, but it's like sitting in a box and hearing noise which just gets louder without warning.

You sort of duck or flinch each time the gust hits; there's no need to, it's just a reflex – proof we aren't relaxed anymore. And we're not talking; we're just sitting and staring.

Category 4 with sustained winds of 145 miles an hour guarantees you won't relax.

But not to talk?

Not even to smile at each other sometimes. No, we're not relaxed. We're tired and uneasy and worried.

How fast is 145 mph? Thinking about a NASCAR race doesn't help you imagine 145 mph. This isn't a car moving at 145 driven by a sports hero, this is the whole world outside doing it, driven by a maniac! And I thought 'That loud, constant banging on our roof must be the solar panels; they're flapping up and down'.

Up and down, up and down, up and down.

'And that sounds like something else hit the house and it's probably Frank's roof tiles, or at least one of them'. (Fortunately he has a lot more left for later).

Anti-hurricane roof tiles might have been a good idea.

And Laura suddenly pointed

'Look at the window!'

I must admit to not realizing what she said since with the shutters up you can't see out of the window.

But she said look **at** it, not through it and, as we looked at it, we could see our beautiful colonial-style window bowing in by three or four inches and then being sucked out again by three or four inches.

'Gosh that's interesting' I thought; the wind is getting behind the shutters and the pressure is causing the window to bow. And they say glass doesn't bend. But is it the glass that's bending, or is the glass remaining rigid and is it the frames that are bending? (You can see physics everywhere if you but take the time to look.) The noise is rather worrying, though.

Constant wind and gusts and bangs make you worry, especially if you can't see out.

Good grief!

What if the window breaks?

Glass coming at my family at 145 miles an hour! I'll never get them to the hospital! How do I deal with that? Where's the first aid kit? Come on Tone! Think!

The window is bending!

But it hasn't smashed yet. It hasn't smashed yet. It hasn't smashed.

I jumped up.

'GET IN THE CLOSET!'

'NOW!'

'GET IN THE CLOSET!'

Life in the closet

It's very small.

I'd always thought of our closet as being quite a big closet because it holds all of Carol's clothes (and a couple of my things). But when you add three fully clothed adults it gets very full very quickly. Even if we'd hung our clothes up it would have been just as full. So we sat for a while just looking into space. The constant bang, bang, bang, the continuous freight train sound, the unending pressure of wondering what was happening and worrying about the big colonial window were beginning to take their toll.

And then I thought 'if the roof rating system is accurate, we should have lost it about 15mph ago.' I don't know what losing a roof sounds like but I do know the scuttle hole cover in the ceiling was heaving on the bolts we'd installed. The draught of the wind in the roof space was sucking the cover as hard as it could. I tried not to look up so Carol and Lor wouldn't have anything else to worry about but I did want to see if it looked like it was holding or if the screws were coming loose.

I must admit to imagining that when your roof comes off it makes a lot of noise. Now don't get me wrong, we had NOISE. Solar panels make a flapping, bang, bang, bang. Roof tiles make a rapid bang, bang, bang (one bang per tile, I guess). And our pool cage made an amazing amount of noise as it twisted and turned before apparently diving into the pool.

And there's a constant "tree-swishing" noise.

And a constant water-from-a-hosepipe and gravel-throwing noise.

And still the wind noise.

And I don't just mean noise, I mean NOISE!

And then it went quite quiet and I thought

'Aaah, it's the end.'

Good thing I didn't pay to watch it because it didn't last very long and you can't see out anyway.

'I'm going back into the garage and see what I can see.'

'Why?'

'Why do you think?'

Well, most of the little windows were broken. The plastic hurricane thingy wasn't so that was money well spent and I stood there. Looking. Good grief it's a mess. Carol just stood. Laura just stood. All just looking.

One of the big trees on the traffic island in front of our house was down and Joan's mum's pool cage was down (I hope her mum understands and doesn't shout at Joan for not being careful with her stuff).

And there were lots of things just lying about in the road, roof tiles, roof shingles, tree branches, cables (no TV for us for a while), black stuff, green stuff, stuff I didn't recognize. The only thing not lying in the road was the port-a-potty that was on next door's front yard. That was just gone.

And I thought

'Well if that's gone through his front window he'll be pissed' (as it were).

And then guess what? Yes, the wind started blowing again. The tree branches started swishing around, the roof shingles started sliding across the road, the cables started whipping up and down and around and around and the things I didn't recognize started to slide and jump and tumble and Lor said

'Let's get back in the closet!'

We tried to be polite and say "After you." But we really wanted to be back in the closet as quickly as possible. And being a dad and a husband meant I was last in and got told off for not getting back in sooner. But I did get back into the closet as soon as I could and I was only a megapixel behind the other two.

But when wives and daughters are worried about you they tell you off. I never understood that aspect of human psychology but have learned to live with it. Now believe you me, the wind was even louder and gustier than the first time and after a bit of thinking more about the roof not being there I thought well the quiet few minutes we spent looking out of the garage window must have been the eye of the storm. Or as Dr Steve would say, "The eye". Being an expert he abbreviates things.

And it got very loud, and then frighteningly loud.

Lying-between-the-tracks-under-a-freight-train loud.

What with the wind and the bangs and bumps it actually got so loud we just looked at each other.

Fear puts a strange look on your face.

Carol and Laura looked amazed. I think I did as well but I couldn't see.

But I could feel. My stomach sort of ached. I got that sharp pain in my chest I've always got when I'm stressed. I knew I was stressed, I just didn't know how I looked.

And then it got quiet again.

And it got warm.

The electricity went off while Dr Steve was saying it's not going north anymore. That was over an hour ago and I'd just started to notice the warmth. Over an hour ago!

It was a long and strange hour.

Fortunately, we had already got torches. (Check) So we had some at the ready for use in case of emergency.

And this was an emergency!

When the electricity goes off it takes the air conditioning with it (A/C for budding experts). Even though it's dark and wet and windy outside it stays hot. Being August. Interestingly without air conditioning it gets quite hot inside. And dark. No light from the light bulbs and still no light through the windows.

'Well now what do we do?' I thought.

So I counted all my fingers and toes. Don't know why, really, but I saw a nurse do it on television during a program about babies and she said it was important for mothers to know. So I thought it was probably also important for fathers to know, so I counted them and they all seemed to be there. But I had to guess some of my toes because I had thick socks on.

I've always liked my toes. They're longer than most people's toes and my second toe is longer than my big toe which makes me a bit like a Neanderthal man because Neanderthal men (and women, probably) had a longer second toe, so it probably makes me a living fossil throw-back thingy. I wonder if I've got Neanderthal genes? I think my dad had Neanderthal genes; he could wiggle his ears. He would sit there and his ears would move; it was dead cool. When we were kids we used to get other kids to come into our house and my dad would wiggle his ears and we'd all giggle. He pretended he didn't know what we were giggling at.

So anyway, I went to the garage door windows and the big tree was still there in the traffic island but it was lying around the other way.

There were more tree branches strewn around, more tiles and shingles and things I didn't recognize.

What a mess. What an awful mess. Actually, "mess" isn't a big enough word. What a dreadful scene. What a dreadful, unbelievable, hurtful scene!

And then we went outside.

We waived to our neighbors because we hadn't seen them for a couple of hours. And we all walked around saying "Hello" and hugging and then we looked and pointed and stared.

I looked at my neighbor's to see if the port-a-potty was there. His front door was smashed, wide open. Fortunately, his house isn't fully built, yet, so no one lives there. Also fortunately, there was no sign of the port-a-potty.

What a mess.

Our front porch was gone; the front porch doors were sticking into the front of the house (some of the bangs and thumps we'd heard). The pool cage was a giant Chinese puzzle toy. The pool screens were shredded. Our beautiful jacaranda trees were down.

The roof was still on but missing lots and lots of shingles. The nice white paint on the walls was peppered with roof tiles and shingle scrapes. The satellite dish was nowhere and the local channels antenna was imitating the pool cage. But being a much more simple piece of household equipment it was very easy to work out which bit was twisted around what.

'I'll not be cleaning my car for a while' I thought. Always wanted a Cadillac and now I've got the worst looking Cadi in existence; or at least the worst looking one that's not actually got a tree lying on it.

We'd all still got all our fingers and toes, so we felt very relieved that our friends and neighbors were merely stirred, not shaken. But everyone's house was shaken. Where did all those roof tiles go? Where did all those green ones come from? Honestly, we don't have any neighbors on any of the local streets with a green roof. Where on earth did they come from?

'You're looking worn out, Jim.'

'Yeah, we nearly lost the front door.' He said in a kind of dazed way

'What? The door? What do you mean?'

'The locks nearly gave way. We dragged the piano over and pushed it up against it and held on.'

'Good grief! Our window bowed in and out but your door?' I was astounded.

'And with my back; well, you know.'

'I'm so sorry, Jim!'

'It's OK; we survived. But I guess we need a new door.'

'I guess so. Go and rest, my friend. Can we bring you anything?'

'No, we're fine. See you tomorrow.'

'Take care, Jim. See you tomorrow.'

Where did all of the debris come from?

Where did our beautiful street go to?

Crying and hugging. Standing and looking. Walking in slow circles around the street and pointing. Looking at each of our roofs but not really noticing details.

So many tree branches and trash bins and roof tiles and sheets of shingles.

So many things that didn't look like anything at all, just junk.

I felt like something I didn't recognize and couldn't describe. Carol put her hand in mine. I put my arm around Laura's shoulder. She had her arms folded and looked very pale.

We went in again and sat on the sofa and spent a quiet evening feeling very tired.

And very dull.

And very sad.

And more dull.

And more sad.

And quiet.

And we thought our own thoughts and looked at each other and smiled and held hands and gave each other hugs.

And sighed.

And then we went to bed.

Tired and dull and sad.

None of the above

How do you know when it's time to get out of bed?
1 It's light
2 The birds are singing
3 Your wife says she wants a cup of coffee
4 All of the above.

Today wasn't going to be an *all of the above* day.

It wasn't really light even though it should have been; no birds were singing and there should have been. Not even our neighborly hawk, who doesn't sing he just sits in our tree and shrieks. I always thought it was because he's not a morning bird and he's telling the larks (who are morning birds) to put a sock in it. No larks, either, no jays, come to think of it. No squirrels running across the roof looking for peanuts to bury.

And Carol was sleeping like a baby.

But it was still time to get up – early.

Lots to do.

Feeling strange.

Why wasn't today an *all of the above* day?

What was missing?

What was different?

What really happened, yesterday?

Why was I sad?

There weren't going to be any stores open in Punta Gorda; that was for sure. And no telephone lines and no gasoline and no television and no radio to check on how things are and no lots of stuff, I suppose.

Feeling strange walking around. No coffee, no tea, no breakfast. There's so much I should be doing.

What should I do?

We NEED things, Tone, we need help, our neighbors need help.

None of us prepared as well as we should have done, I know that, now. We bought water and batteries and some tarps and stuff and put up our hurricane shutters, just like the booklets tell us to but now it's obvious that wasn't enough. It wasn't enough! Confound it, it wasn't enough! Oh, how I wish I could have a last week do-over, again. I'd better make a list and find a store.

So, off to find a store before anyone else is awake, to buy some after-the-hurricane-stuff.

'Venice is the best bet.' I thought. I like Venice; it's one of those comfortable towns. We love Venice Beach, the pier, the sand, the hot dog guy. The warm, calm feeling you get in Venice is one of the reasons we came to Florida.

But today I'm sad.

And that's why I'm sad. Our home. Our street. Our neighbors' homes.

They're not like they were yesterday morning. They're like they are **this** morning. After-the-hurricane mornings aren't a bit like an *all of the above* day.

'Shape up', Tone. Venice here I come! In Carol's van. I can get more in the back of the van than I can in the Cadillac.

That's sensible. Well done, Tone. Keep thinking like that.

Garage door opens OK and it's not as heavy as I'd expected (once I'd released the drive chain) It's not possible to push it open with the drive chain engaged! I'll remember that for next time.

Shut up, Tone, there ain't gonna be no next time.

Broken glass falling out of the little windows. Sweep it up. Don't want a puncture.

Back out. Drive off. Watch what you do. What's the best way to get to the Interstate? Slowly and carefully, that's the best way. Driving through hurricane debris doesn't lend itself to high speed and listening to music at the same time. It's like driving on a flooded road or on broken glass. Or ice. You don't just go slow, you go careful. You will the car to stay moving. You feel every possible nail or damaged cable hoping that you won't get a flat. You don't quite sit in the seat, you sort of hover above it. You break more carefully. You watch all your mirrors.

This is not an all of the above day at all.

It's a *never-before* day.

I can't get through. What **is** all that stuff? They've barricaded the road.

No they haven't. It's buildings. Good grief it's the town homes. This is all town home! Roofs, walls, drapes, everything in piles all across the road.

Those poor people!

I have to turn round. I'll go the other way, there's no way I'm getting through on this road. This is incredible!

Where is everybody?

Why am I the only car on the road?

Has the Sheriff closed all the roads?

Am I breaking the law?

Am I being stupid being out on the road? Where is everybody? I'm scared.

I shouldn't be but I am. Not scared, exactly, I feel kind of guilty I've just not been caught yet. I feel so uneasy about this.

Great God in Heaven! Their roof's totally gone! So's theirs!

It's two streets away and these houses look like they've been bombed. Just like the town homes. It's a flaming war zone. This is madness. What on earth am I doing out on my own? Why is my roof still on when they've all lost theirs? Tornadoes! We got the eye, they got the eye wall. They got the tornadoes! Blood and sand! Nothing can stand up to a tornado! And we missed it by a couple of streets.

There's someone! I'm not alone!

There's someone else!

It's not *Day of The Triffids*.

But it **is** like a funeral procession. Everyone is driving at 15mph. Everywhere is trashed. Junk and trash and tree branches and cables and poles. And whole sheets of plywood with shingles on them. These are people's roofs in the street; people's *homes*!

What is this place we used to call "home"?

Let I75 be open!

Just let that Interstate be open! Please let it be open!

That's the EMS building's roof! It's the whole flaming roof lying there! They lost the roof!

It's open! I can see headlights moving across the overpass. But there aren't any traffic lights. There aren't any traffic light poles. There's just debris.

Debris you weave around; it's like driving drunk, except I'm going all over the road on purpose so I don't hit a light pole or something. Good grief what is this mess we used to call home?

Get to Venice, Tone. There's work to be done. There and back before Carol and Laura wake up!

There and back, safe and sound.

Think, Tone, think!

I didn't leave a note telling them where I am. Oh for crying out loud, why didn't I leave a note? You've got to get back before they wake up.

Who's that? What the? Who are they?

Five or six men ahead of me. All in black. They look like bandit (the word didn't get spoken). They're directing traffic. They're National Guard or something. They've actually shipped in law enforcement.

There's more of them. Every corner of every road. Green uniforms. Black uniforms. Look at the guns, these guys mean business.

It was days before anyone got to Homestead after Hurricane Andrew. Wow! They're *here*. At least we'll be crime-free. Thanks Jeb!

'Yes, Sir.'

'Venice.'

'I need supplies for my family.'

'Yes, Sir.'

'Thank you'.

I even saluted him. I don't know why; it just felt right. Something between gratitude and respect, between feeling vulnerable because of yesterday and strong because they're all here.

Up to the slip road. More Guardsmen. Waving me through.

'Thank you'. I shouted.

Onto the interstate. That's the cell phone tower, or what's left of it. Rather like a giant version of our local channels antenna. Oh no, look at all the pines and crap just strewn about. I'll never get to Venice. Oh God, what if I'm stuck in the road? It'll take an hour to walk back home. Oh, this is stupid, Tony. Why did you do such a thing?

This is crazy!

It's normal again.

I've been driving for fifteen minutes and the roads are clear! I'm doing 70mph! It's surreal; back there it's a nightmare and just up here it's normal! What kind of hurricane was that?

Venice is a nice town. And this is a very nice store – open, serving customers, cool. And everyone is saying how relieved they are that the hurricane didn't hit. They don't know I'm from "down there", "Charlotte", "Hurricane Highway". They've got names for us already. They've already separated us off from the normal world. We're "them" and it's a very unnerving feeling.

Home improvement store, handyman store, building supplies store where are you? There! Get what you need and go. What do I need?

Why didn't I write a proper list before I set off? Why didn't I look at the house and my neighbors' houses to see what we all might need? Why wasn't I thinking straight?

This is stupid; our homes have been destroyed, nearly, and I just drove off without even bringing a pencil, let alone a proper list of things to take back. I can't phone anyone to check anything.

Oh Tony. You fool.

Walk the aisles and get what you need and what you might need and what the neighbors might need. And then go home. Just spend money before they run out of supplies, I can't be the only one of "them" to come here.

And phone England; tell them we won't be phoning for a while because we don't have phone service.

I don't know how to use a public payphone!

I've never called international on a payphone. I don't even know if I've got enough money. What kind of preparation did I do for this hurricane?

'Hello. Yes, I've got a credit card. Yes, charge the card. Thank you operator, thank you.'

Please be in, son. Please be in.

'Ey up, Mate.'

'Yeah, fine.'

'Bit of a mess but don't worry. We're all safe.'

'Venice.'

'Shopping; I need more tarps and stuff. I'm going to get more rope. And duct tape and bungee cords and –

No, we've still got a roof but, yes, there's been damage.

No, we're fine, I just don't want it to rain in.'

'I never thought of that. Thanks. Plastic sheeting and a staple gun. How did you think of that?'

Because that's what animals do; they climb up high to be safe. Our roof is high. They'll get in through the soffits. You're brilliant, son, you really are.

'Great, thanks – roach killer; of course they'll come in; where they live has been destroyed, so they'll look for somewhere safe'.

Blimey, I never thought of that – we'll be inundated with bugs and vermin.

'Yes, I'll get more food and water. Chocolate? OK, chocolate. I've got beer.'

'Yeah'.

'Take care'.

'Love you, too'.

'Call Auntie Audrey and Grandma Sylvia in case I can't get through.'

'Thanks. What? Did I put the radio on? Why? I doubt it; but OK I'll turn it on when I head back.'

'Love you.'

'Have I turned the radio on?' I mumbled to myself, as I climbed back in the van. 'What a question! Anyway I said I would. I'll do it when I get closer; Seaview doesn't come this far.'

So I bought myself a coffee and started back down I75. Personally I didn't feel like any more sound, noise, whatever. I knew what was waiting for me just a half hour drive away. But I said I would.

'104.9 it is, son.' I said to myself as though we were still talking to each other. You've got to be kidding me! Seaview is broadcasting! I don't believe it. They sound shattered; their voices are powerful, determined, but there's so much emotion. What? They lost the roof! They had to save their lives but were back on the air within four hours! Four hours! Unbelievable! Our radio station is broadcasting already. Those people are heroic.

And then it was drive back to the untidy part, to "down there", to "Charlotte", to "Hurricane Highway" to see if it was as bad as I thought it was when I left.

Yes, it is as bad as I thought it was when I left. Blood and sand! What a mess!

Got home safe and sound, though, and unloaded all the tarps and nails and ropes and bungee cords and furring strips and propane tanks.

I don't feel so screwdriver-challenged as I did before.

'Dad, I want to go to look at my condo. I want to see my home. I want to check the damage.'

'Of course, Sweetheart. Thank you for being so wonderful.'

'Got to, Father! Stiff upper lip and all that.' She said as she put on her daft, upper class, English accent.

'I love you, Sweetheart. Only you could make me laugh today.'

So I got into the driver's seat and we drove down 42nd Street – in my Cadillac. Good car to drive – after a hurricane. We didn't really go down 42nd Street and in Bob Dylan's version it was a war but I've always wanted to say that. Now I get the chance.

'Dad! The place looks like a war zone! Just look! Look at the utility poles, Look at the trees. Look at the lamp posts lying across the road. Look at the traffic lights. Dad! Don't drive over those cables! Watch out for those garbage cans. Dad, it's awful!'

'Yeah, I know, Sweetheart, I was out, earlier.'

'So you were.' Well done, Father'. She said, regaining that amazing composure of hers.

There were a lot of sad people around, now.

'Sweetheart, be prepared for the worst.'

'I am.'

Drove into the condo units. Missing roofs, missing gables, missing walls.

(Let Laura's home be alright!)

'Good Grief!'

How can this be? It's a miracle! Not so much as a spoon out of place. Who's your Daddy? Everything just as they were left. Apart from the tarps over the furniture it's as though she was never away.

'Oh! I'm so happy for you, Sweetheart!'

'Why is there water in the bedroom, Dad?'

'Window must have leaked. You can see the stains round the frame. The wall's soaked, you can see it.'

'Dad, there's a dripping sound in the laundry room.'

'Next door must have a leak, can't see anything wrong here. But just to be safe let's drive round to look at the back of the condo'.

'Can't get through – too much rubble and standing water. We'll go another day.'

'I want to go, now.'

'Of course you do. We'll walk. We just have to get far enough round to be able to see the roof.'

'Let's get the tarps off the furniture, first because we have some roof work to do back at the grande hacienda and perhaps I didn't buy enough in Venice. And the neighbors will need some, probably.'

'Be careful where you walk. Do NOT even get close to those cables. And don't paddle through the puddles, there might be a cable lying in it. Electricity and water will kill us.'

The only thing worse than seeing a great gaping hole in your roof is seeing a great gaping hole in your daughter's roof. That's where the water is coming from. Half the roof is gone. At least it's just the roof, itself. Look at that one; it's lost its gable-end and half the wall.

'Dad, why isn't there more water in my condo if the roof's

damaged?'

'I think, because you've got poured concrete ceiling and walls. Your place is built like a fortress – except for the roof trusses and shingles, that's what failed, the rest is OK. But the water that came in has to go somewhere, so that's why we can hear dripping. It's finding its way down behind the drywall. I'm afraid you'll not be able to move back for a while.'

'That's OK. Why did that other building lose its gable end?'

'Because the later buildings had a lot more frame construction; yours was one of the first buildings to go up and they used poured concrete.

'Lucky old you!'

"Lucky!" Lucky used to mean winning the lottery; now it means not having your home totally destroyed. Definitely a *none of the above* day.

A man's gotta do …

'What to do? What to do?'

Pretty obvious, really.

The roof.

So now it's a case of get on the roof, nail down the tarps to ensure "weather-proofity" and then we can set about doing everything else.

I've never been on a roof.

Ever.

Roofs are high up.

Still, a man's gotta do what his wife won't.

Now then – how to get up there? How do you get up on a roof?

How do you send a sixty year-old man up on a roof and return him once again safely to earth? (As JFK might have said.)

Fortunately, I spent some of my teenage years listening to Mr.

Boland in a physics lab. After three long years of high school physics I graduated with what today would be considered a fail. (Actually, it was a "fail" then, as well) Yet, strangely, the experience left me with three essential pieces of knowledge.

#1 Mr. Boland didn't like me very much.

Example – we were once doing specific gravity (which is very complicated) and he said 'Does anyone have any questions?'

and I said 'Can I have an ice cream?'

Physics teachers just don't have a sense of humor.

#2 If you're actually on a roof and you fall off it's possible to calculate your very own ground-impact velocity. For budding physics experts you use the formula $V2 - U2 = 2gs$ (V is final velocity and g is something to do with gravity). The formula is based on Newton's First Law of Specific Gravity which states (apparently) *The higher the roof the more it will hurt.*

And #3 is to get on a roof you have to use an anti-gravity device (or AGD for physicists). My AGD of choice is the step ladder. Also known as an "up quark" if you're reading this in CERN. (CERN's a place not a language).

So on with the old cycle helmet – falling off a roof can be less painful if you're wearing a cycle helmet (One of my laws).

The roof is quite steep – but not so steep that it exceeds the co-efficient of friction (and they said I learned nothing in physics lessons). And it's very hot. Until you get on a roof in Florida, you have no idea how hot a roof can be.

You can't put your hand on it, you can't sit on it, you can't kneel on it, you can't rest your elbow on it and if you stand up on it, you're too far away to knock a nail in it.

Then Laura came up on the roof. She didn't even notice it was high or steep or hot, so I had to pretend it wasn't high or steep or hot, so now not only did I suffer a hurricane and not only did I have to confront a screwdriver and not only do I have to relive my physics lessons, but now I have to climb on a roof and get sunburned and be scared and not let my daughter know.

It's not going to be a quiet Saturday out of the office, either.

Have you ever knocked nails through four tarpaulins into a hot, steep, scary roof the day after a really scary hurricane?

Well, stop judging me!

And half the time the nails are too far away from where you are and you have to go back, because how do you ask your daughter to go and get them when you've got nothing to hold on to anyway and the wind starts blowing (and after a hurricane and the wind starts blowing you don't know if it is coming back)? So, as well as hot and steep and scary and nowhere to hold on to, you've got wind as well that might not stop.

And those flaming tarps billow out like sails. I'm on a stupid roof, I'm scared, I'm tired, I'm trying to look brave and I'm fighting 400 square feet of flying tarp!

Sometimes it's really tough being a dad.

But we (mainly Laura) finished hammering what seemed like a million nails into what also seemed like 400 tarpaulins. To say nothing of what seemed like several miles of furring strips.

And each tarp just loved catching the wind!

By the way – you lie on one bit of the tarp and nail it down, then you slide down a bit and knock in another nail and then, when you've got it tamed, you nail a furring strip down and the tarp knows who's in charge.

But it ain't easy!

And it ain't fast!

(But it is hot and steep and scary.)

After a couple of hours of hard labor, it seemed like we had covered all the black bits on the roof where the shingles had gone absent without leave. We had consumed pints of warm water and suffered what felt like heat stroke, sun burn and vertigo.

And crushed thumbs. I'm not good with hammers, either.

Laura looked as fresh as a daisy and after helping me down while Carol steadied the anti-gravity device (in case I slipped) she said 'Right, then; what's next?'

'What's next?'

'Are you kidding me?'

It really is hard being a dad, sometimes.

But I responded with a jaunty smile and said

'Race you to collect all the fallen shingles, tiles, branches, bits of pool cage, plastic bags, cups and saucers, car tires, things I don't recognize and old Marvin Rainwater records, as well as anything else we might find strewn around.'

'OK.' She said as if she was still warming up before doing some real work.

Anyway not many people have ever heard of Marvin Rainwater and very few people ever seemed interested enough to collect any of his records. His biggest hit "I Gotta Go Get My Baby" never really made it to the top of the Country Music charts but, yes, I still own a copy even though I never play it; never even hum it to myself and I certainly don't remember what was on the 'B' side. It might be "Daddy's Glad You Came Home" but perhaps not.

Anyway, stroke of genius, I agreed that I would search diligently for Marvin Rainwater records and Laura would pick up all the other stuff since it would be of less value and it wouldn't matter too much if she were to drop anything on her way to the mounting pile of storm debris being assembled on the front lawn. And everyone else's front lawns. We were a labor gang, picking and hauling and piling. At least someone, I think Ellery, suggested we pile similar things together to make it easier for trash collection. So we were roofs and general crap, the vacant lot was trees and tree branches. And so on and so on.

I decided my search might benefit from some planning (plans are nothing, planning is everything) and so I sat in the garage on a deck chair and planned my search.

And rested!

And ached!

And felt a little like a failure for resting.

Well while I was planning and Laura was picking and moving it seems that my better half had donned a wet suit, strapped on her sub aqua gear, armed herself with a harpoon gun (in case of biting fish) and was in the deep end of the pool manhandling lumps of roof, screen cage, shingles, soffits and lanai furniture to the surface as part of "Operation Pool Clean Up".

Things at the bottom of a pool seem much smaller when viewed from the surface but, apparently, they achieve normal size as one approaches the pool bottom. And normal weight when one raises said items to the pool surface. Photons can do that.

I wonder if that's because the photons get squashed a bit by the weight of the water of if they just pretend to, so that you'll think cleaning out a pool will be a bit of a doddle. Physics is fascinating. I bet Newton has a Law about it. Plus which, because water is eight hundred times as dense as air it affects how you breathe. When under water (Carol didn't really have a wet suit or sub aqua gear) your breathing is reduced by 50%. – you can breathe out but you can't breathe in. For some reason fish aren't affected by this property of water.

Anyway after much planning (and resting and feeling like a failure) I decided that something the size of a 45 rpm record could easily be hidden by broken shingles or something and so the efficient way to locate lost records might be to move stuff and see if there's anything underneath.

Hours and hours later you have big piles of debris on the front lawn and fatigue sets in and you get really slow until you nearly stop moving and you have to lie down just to stop the fatigue from hurting.

Terms like bone-weary and dog-tired begin to have real meaning.

After the second day of debris collecting (yes, it's now Sunday!) I think the only part of my body that doesn't hurt is my hair. And even though we had cleaned up almost the entire surface area of what we call "our bit" not a single Marvin Rainwater record had been sighted, let alone retrieved.

Operation "Keep Cleaning Stuff Up Even Though It Will Take Forever" was in full swing. Frank and Roger were cleaning up, Jim and Shirley were cleaning up, everyone was cleaning up.

By Monday the street seemed to be one long pile of crap, junk, tree branches, and stuff no one recognized. Florida without air conditioning and without electric lights and without a refrigerator to put your head in and without a television (which, apparently, works off the same electricity as everything else) to look at can get very hot and sweaty and smelly. It took two days just to get water in the house out of a tap. Before then we were having to spray ourselves with a spray bottle and rub very fast with soap.

But because our water pipe had been broken by a hose pipe (I didn't think of bringing the hose in, so during the hurricane it must have whipped around and it yanked on the water pipe until it cracked). So now the water just kept spraying out through the break instead of coming in to the house like it's supposed to.

So since I was off sick the day all the other kids in my class learned how to do plumbing I put Plan B into effect. Fortunately I used to be a Boy Scout (dyb dyb dyb) and can do knots. So I got some hemp rope (it gets tighter when it's wet) and did a square lashing round the broken pipe. I also wrapped the pipe with "plumber's tape". "Plumber's tape" is not what I called it before I immigrated and became a foreigner. To an English plumbing expert it's known as PTFE tape. And the only reason I mention that is because in between failing physics I also failed chemistry but, to my continuing pleasure, I am one of the few people in the world who know that PTFE stands for polytetrafluoroethylene.

And it worked like a charm.

The pipe is fixed and the water stayed in it. But just to be safe we turned the water off at the mains when we weren't having a shower or shaving. Shaving in cold water is rather infra dig but at least no one from my old school could see me.

Now, here's something else you learn after a hurricane, showering in cold water is absolute bliss. 90+ degrees of heat, hard work, just as hot and humid inside as out and then – aaaaah! A cold shower.

I found the best way to wash clothes was to wear them in the shower and wash them like Cary Grant did in "Charade" and then take them off (as Cary Grant didn't) and shower the rest of me. OK, you still have to step out of the shower into hot-and-humid world. But for a brief moment there's solitude, and peace, and coolness. And being still, even for just a few minutes, is bliss.

I'm telling you, until you've been afraid and dull and sad and bone-weary tired and scared and worried about your wife and daughter and your neighbors you don't really know how wonderful it is to be still and cool.

Cold water running over my aching body.

Thank you, God.

Generator world

Two days without water.

Four days without air conditioning.

Four days without television.

But four days with pain and fatigue and worry and sadness.

And a little bewilderment.

When I say "without water" I don't mean NO water at all. I mean water from two miles away (if you're lucky) given out by young guys in military uniform carrying very big assault rifles asking you to take "just one, sir" as you get to the front of the line. A gallon jug of water. A pack of supermarket bottled water.

'Just one, sir.' With a smile (and a big gun).

Too tired to argue and too sad to care.

"Just one" is fine. I can always go back to the end of the line and start again. Well after I get a hat. I always forget to wear a hat and it's always so sunny. Bald heads should be banned in Florida. I hate wearing a hat. Sun burned bald heads should definitely be banned in Florida.

Anyway, enough water for a while. It's amazing, no appetite at all but unquenchable thirst. We are all working like Trojans, hour after hour, but don't have any appetite. Life after a hurricane is very strange.

I worked out why we're never hungry. We work too hard. All the blood goes to your skin to help you sweat so it's not deep in your gut. That means your body can't digest food so you don't want to eat. Hunger adds to fatigue but your body won't take in food. But it takes in lots and lots and lots of water. The official gallon per person per day which you buy before the storm (have three days-worth in stock) is **not** enough.

Here it is Day 4 and we don't have any water. And we're drinking it like we were camels. And we drive miles to get some and stand in line in the hot sun and get only as many as we're allowed.

We could have planned a bit better than this.

'Thank you.' I say as I take the water and head back to the car.

'Any ice?'

'No, sir, no ice. Maybe tomorrow. They're trucking it in from Tampa.'

Tampa! We got their hurricane and now we get their ice.

That's fair.

I have to do something. I have to make ice.

And then I thought 'Buy a generator!' With a generator you can power the whole house. We'll have ice, air conditioning, television, hot showers. When you have air conditioning you always have hot showers (unless you are a teenage boy and your dad tells you to take a cold shower).

Now then. Since I was also off sick the day they did generator power at our school I decided to get some expert advice from Ellery.

Ellery knows stuff.

Ellery is one of those men you would most want to be cast away with on a desert island. Not because he can cook or do housework or anything but because he knows how to survive; he's, well, practical. So off I went to Ellery's house.

And I said

'I'm thinking of getting a generator, can you give me some advice?'

'Good idea' he said. 'Can you get one for me?'

'What sort should I get?'

'Whatever sort they've got.'

'What do you mean *whatever sort they've got?*'

'They'll have whatever is in stock, just get whatever they have.'

'Sounds like good advice' I thought.

Then Ellery changed his mind and decided he didn't want a generator. A seed of doubt was now sown. If Ellery doesn't want a generator perhaps I don't want a generator. Ellery knows more about generators than I do.

But I have to tell you I was in great need of feeling good about something and so I threw caution to the wind and asked Carol to come with me to help (after I'd said the magic word).

Carol and I drove through the storm-tossed, debris-strewn streets of "Sadtown" to that home and garden and contractor supply store and got in line. This place is a bit like Office Depot except they don't sell anything I understand. But it seems that buying a generator requires that you wait in line with a hundred other people waiting for the big truck to arrive from where ever, bringing which ever kind of generators they happen to have. I'm encouraged by the thought that if all these people want a generator then it must be right; many of them look knowledgeable about such things.

'You wait in line, my dear,' I said to my wife and partner in this expedition into the unknown, 'I am going to find a generator expert.'

Actually she said 'I'll wait I line and you go and get the water you left in the van.'

Now that's not because I don't know how to wait in line properly it's because the line was air conditioned and I left the water in the van shortly after she told me to make sure I brought it with us. (I always was forgetful; this failing is because I'm "me" not because I'm post-hurricane "me".) Anyway, on my way to the van I bumped into a guy with a "How Can I Help?" on his shirt. And he clearly looked like he knew more than enough to teach me. And I learned that generators have engines like little cars but they don't go anywhere, you start them by pulling a rip cord, like a walk-behind lawn mower but they don't cut grass, they don't like to be on all day and must have their oil changed every so many hours of operation.

And another interesting thing about them is that they don't plug into the house and you can't run your air conditioning off them because they just don't have enough "umph", to use a technical expression.

But they will run fans and a refrigerator and lamps and the television.

And they are so loud that after a day or so you will have damaged your hearing so much you will shout at everybody all the time. (That doesn't matter too much unless you are a secret agent or you're sitting in the confessional talking to your priest).

And they are the heaviest thing you will ever attempt to pick up. Ever. Fortunately the man at the store helped me lift it into the back of the van for which I was so grateful. By the time we got home, however, he had disappeared and, it seemed, so had Carol.

Carol knows me so well that without even discussing it she went to Frank's house to get help. Roger, Frank's son-in-law, is even more capable than Ellery and he now lives closer.

Not close enough, though, because by the time he arrived on the scene carrying something known as a socket set I'd lifted the generator out of the van and onto the driveway. Remembering words like 'moments about a point' and 'fulcrum' I'd been able to achieve what the man in the store said was impossible. But since he'd not bothered to run alongside until we got home I had little choice other than to open the box and remove the gas-powered generator single-handedly or to ask someone for help. I'm a man and men don't ask for help. What else do I have to tell you. (Other than I don't recommend lifting those things up single-handedly.)

'I could have helped you do that' said Roger 'in fact I don't believe you just lifted that thing out on your own even though I saw you do it.'

'Well believe' I said, trying not to pant, 'I'm going to read the instructions, once I've found the English version'.

Whenever I pick up an instruction booklet I always think of that amazing book about motorcycle maintenance. There's a line in it where the hero is commenting on his not very practical friend's attitude to all things mechanical.

First adopt a quiet state of mind he says.

I always want to adopt a quiet state of mind but when instructions are written in six languages in columns down a double page and they all point to the same diagrams my mind becomes very unquiet.

I shouldn't feel defeated by diagrams just because they are supported by six different languages but I do. And the first line I can read states that to assemble the unit (I always skip the line congratulating me on the purchase, by the way) I only need a screwdriver.

A screwdriver!

I know that isn't true.

It is never true.

It was written down by mistake in the first instruction book ever published in six different languages and it has appeared in instruction books ever since.

The sole purpose of the screwdriver statement is to defeat me.

I'm hungry, hot, tired, in pain, sad, embarrassed because I can't read instruction books and I don't really know what a socket set is, I'm in the middle of my driveway where everyone can see me and a man who has just had his home totally destroyed by Hurricane Charley is standing next to me with a socket set in his hand looking calm and compassionate and ready to help me.

'This is how you assemble it.' He said. 'You won't need the manual.'

And with that he put the wheels on and the little legs on and the handle on and he gave me some straps because they're not needed (who knew?) and he filled it with oil and he said 'You put the gas in there.'

Then he went back to Frank's house because he hasn't got anywhere else to live. And I felt so cared for.

There goes a man who has lost his home. He had to get out of it while it fell about his and his wife's heads, get in a truck and drive through a Category 4 hurricane to the only safe place they knew. And I just know he will be more tired and more sad and more in pain than I am and yet he has just assembled a generator he will never benefit from.

And I said a very quiet and very heartfelt thank you to him as he walked away.

And I looked proudly at my new generator. I can now provide comfort for my family. I am a real man again!

And I wheeled my new man-toy to the side of the house, filled it with gas, plugged yellow, green and orange extension cords into it (we use them for Christmas lights), fed them through a window into the house and pulled the rip cord. It roared into life!

My man-toy was now an essential part of our struggle to re-enter the post-modernist era where they have paintings I don't understand and shock jocks I don't care for. But we no longer live in the Third World.

We plugged appliances into it and they all came on.

We were now in the Second World.

Civilized living is no longer just a memory of the past and a hope for the future; civilization is back and it is now.

We hugged.

The refrigerator cooled a little, the fan blew air around a little, the lamp lit the room a little and then we began to shout and I was happy not to be a secret agent or to be meeting with my priest. So I shouted some more.

What will we do with our new-found power? Morning coffee? Toast and marmalade? Television? Cups of tea? Oh tea!

To start with we just sat in front of the fan and said nothing.

And I did think that with the fan on "high" there's no way we'd ever be able to play Monopoly.

Life is good!

And I was the one who made it so.

Well, actually, Roger made it so. All I did was wheel it round the back and pull the rip cord. And since there will be no Monopoly I have the time and the electric light to read the instructions. The hurricane shutters are still up and it is still dark.

Column 1 on all pages appears to be English; the first column should always be English since I was off sick that day as well, I never mastered the other languages and so checking across the page to see what they say would be a trivial pursuit.

I resolved to focus on Column 1, regardless of the page number.

Well what do you know, the man-toy will operate across a whole range of volts and currents up to a maximum wattage of about 6000. I become more and more impressed with my knowledge of things physical the longer I live in the Third World.

If you multiply the volts by the amps you get the watts.

The whats? No, the watts. Another old joke but this time one which rarely gets a laugh, even when told to old physics teachers who have never been to Tampa Bay.

Unfortunately there has to be more to working out watts than that because if you multiply the volts in our house by the amps in the breaker panel you get more than one hundred which is what the light bulb says it is. So rather than doing the math I decided to work empirically and plug in all the stuff we need until the gas ran out and then decide what to do from there. Which, incidentally, would enable me to both adopt a quiet state of mind and come up with an excuse to tell my wife and daughter after stuff stops working.

Life is still good.

Well quite good, my wife and daughter seem firm in their opinion that if I don't know the answer I make it up. It's a good thing they didn't mark my high school homework or I might have graduated everything with a fail.

As Mr. Lincoln said "You can fool some of the people all of the time and you can fool all of the people some of the time but you can't fool wives and daughters any of the time."

Life's still pretty good.

And for the moment I am the hero of generator-power. Tomorrow I will have to go back to Venice, where it's all neat and tidy, and buy more gasoline. And a proper coffee from Hess. And a battery for Laura's car. And more stuff. It's amazing how much stuff you get through when you spend day after day clearing up after a hurricane.

And some more of those fix-a-flat canisters. Until you've been in a hurricane you really have no idea how many flat tires you and your neighbors are going to get. But if anyone ever asks you, the answer is "a lot".

I wonder what Dr Steve and Jim and Lois are doing today?

I wonder if Carol can get the TV to work off gasoline-power?

Back in the First World again

You know how some people achieve greatness and some people have greatness thrust upon them? Well I think my wife was just born great.

I'm sitting there having a relax and trying to memorize the answers on the Community Chest cards from Monopoly and she said

'Voila!'

And I said 'Pardon?'

And she said 'VOI LAAA!'

And I said 'Have you been reading that generator manual in the wrong columns?'

And she said 'VWAAAAA LAAAAAAAA!

And I said 'Look, I can't hear you; can you turn the television down a bit?'

Television?

Turn down the television?

We don't have a television.

Well we do have a television but it doesn't work anymore because we don't have any electricity And then it hit me. The television is working. And I said 'Wow! Do you know what this means? It means I just fixed the television without a screwdriver, just by sitting here!'

That's called telekinesis. Am I good, or what? I wonder if Dr Steve could do that. Although just banging a television with your leg isn't fixing it. I know that in the olden days when all televisions were in black and white and the picture went fuzzy you would give it a bit of a thump and the picture would come back. But that's not what Dr Steve did. He didn't give the monitor a well-placed thump (that hurricane definitely went right a bit, though).

I wonder if Dr Steve's a Sagittarius? I'm a Sagittarius, and I'm also left-handed (more Neanderthal genery) and I bump things I don't mean to.

My mom used to call me clumsy but it's not about being clumsy; it's more esoteric than just being clumsy. It's metaphysical. Whenever you meet someone and they're a bit metaphysical (clumsy) and you say

'Are you a Sagittarius?'

They say 'Yeah. How did you know?'

It's a fact of science, all Sagittarians bump things. I think it's because of their astrological sun sign. Astrology is a branch of metaphysics. (Far more interesting than the ordinary physics they teach in high school). If you think about it, everybody is like their sun sign; Libras are very balanced, Scorpios can be very biting (but not like fish; otherwise they'd be Pisces), Gemini people sort of have two personalities. And it's the same for Sagittarius.

It's a half man and a half horse sign. And that's the problem.

They've got two extra legs.

And that makes it very difficult to co-ordinate. You see people have two legs, not four legs. And so if you're doing a hurricane advisory and you're concentrating on the big swirly thing and you're telling people in Tampa it might be time to duck (also got two legs) and if you just turn a bit and if you don't think about things one of your astrological legs might just bang the monitor screen and how can you say

'Sorry about that, viewers, it was my extra leg.'

You can't can you? You just hope no one noticed and you move on. Well, I noticed, Dr Steve, because it sent Hurricane Charley another fifty miles right.

Now just in case you're trying to keep up I know they're not real legs, they're metaphysical legs. It all started with Julius Caesar in that play about William Shakespeare when he said

"The fault, dear Brutus, is not in ourselves, it is in our stars."

He said it in Latin, of course. (I think he was from Bolivia.)

So, anyway.

'Me Darlin!' I cried, 'Can you believe I got the television to work just by sitting here and doing telekinetics?'

And you don't want to know what she said back but it would have rhymed with "damned thing upside your head". But believe you me, the thrill of returning to the First World was something to be savored. We have television. We have television! We can watch 'The News' and we can watch 'Friends' and I can watch Meredith on 'Millionaire'. But I couldn't be a phone-a-friend because our phones don't work.

And anyway once my better half had got all of my attention she did persuade me (almost) that it was not perhaps mere coincidence that she'd been attaching wires to things to tap into the generator and using rabbits' ears to tap into the ether. It seems that even without electricity the television (oh, that word) signals still keep coming into our house (probably just in case we found our satellite dish and put it back up) so that we could, either telekinetically or more mundanely, pick them up and watch on our television.

Television! Television! Television!

Teleeeeviiiisionnnnn!!

(Say it soft and it's almost like praying.)

Now it seems, according to she-who-was-born-great, that we can only pick up local stations and we will be limited to four or five channels and the video recorder (so no Big Brother and no Meredith. Ah well). Well I can tell you and no mistake that 4 and 5 will now be numbers of choice on my lottery tickets. They are good numbers. And if the video store ever gets its roof back we'll have some very pleasant nights and weekends watching video reruns of popular films which normally run on TCM and AMC. And since we can't spend nights and weekends making unlimited cell phone calls, the TV (Oh!) is all we'll have.

But I don't care. Fan, refrigerator, light, television, generator noise. Life is indeed good (well apart from the generator noise.) I wonder if Carol can fix that. I wonder if I can fix that, in a metaphysical way. I'm going to practice.

I wonder if we can get Dr Steve.

No. Dr Steve is not on local channels. Being in the National Hurricane Center he won't be local. If he'd been local he could have looked out of the window like Lois and Jim did.

And we can now get Lois and Jim and they have a definite "in" when it comes to knowing what's happening on the local meteorological scene.

And with television and a refrigerator and a fan we can pretend that it's not hot and we can begin to live like we used to even though there's still an unbelievable amount of stuff left to pick up.

And isn't it great we have National Guard and firefighters and police from everywhere you've ever seen on television and Red Cross and Tampa ministries and Salvation Army and everyone else directing traffic and handing out food and bottles of water and driving great big back hoes to shift the stuff and FPL people who dig holes and put up new poles, are stringing about a hundred million miles of cable all over the place but still have millions more to do.

And in our little love nest we can turn on the light and turn on the television and drink a cool drink and just forget for a little while that in the outside it's not the same as it used to be.

Except for the ice. Lack of generator umph means we don't manufacture our own ice; we still have to drive a couple of miles and line up and ask the National Guard chaps how many we can have this time.

Wonderfully we have a plan. We and our neighbors talk each day about what we each need and then we take it in turns to go to different places to get the things on the list. Much better than doing it individually. Someone will go to the local strip mall for the handouts, someone else goes into town to Wal-Mart and someone else drives up to Venice. And we all check in on friends who can't drive just to make sure they have what they need, as well. It's rotten going through what we all went through but it really does make you realize just how thoughtful and caring other people are.

Anyway, back to work. I think the list is getting shorter but it doesn't feel that way. We're firing on as many cylinders as we can but my feet hurt and my calves hurt and I forgot to ask whoever went to a pharmacy to get me some magic muscle balm. It's all the step ladder work; those flaming soffits. Climb up, drag the construction grade plastic sheeting behind me, hold it up to the soffit with one hand, punch the staples in with the other. 20 seconds of muscle burn. Climb down, move the step ladder, climb up, drag the sheeting, hold it up, punch the staples. 20 seconds of muscle burn. Climb down. Let my arms go limp, stare at the soffits, move the ladder, climb up. I will never moan about going into the office, ever again. My arms hurt more than my legs. My neck aches. I sweat like a horse.

I'd better do the roof space. The insulation will be all over the place. And I can do it without lifting my arms over my head. And I can get out of the sun.

Oh, it's going to be so hot in there. I've just realized I have a splitting headache. It's hot. I'm tired. My head feels like it's got a steel band wrapped round it. I'm tired of drinking water. I'm tired of heartburn. I'm just tired.

Just tired, that's all. I'll be fine in a minute.

I always meant to tighten those screws. I creak about as much as the pull-down ladder. Blood and sand, look at it; how am I going to push all that fiberglass back. Oh, for crying out loud it's going to take days. It's fiberglass, don't touch it. Go and put long pants on, Tone. And get a mask on. Are you stupid, or what? Climbing onto fiberglass in shorts. Get your head straight and do this properly. For crying out loud, Tony, why don't you just go out and roll around in the cactus. Get your act together, will you!

Back in the roof space, feeling like I'm in an oven. 129°. My goggles have steamed up. I can't see and I've only just got up here. Go back down and tie a scarf round your head and wipe the inside of the goggles. I haven't even started and I want to collapse. I hate this. Why didn't I stand things over the soffits to keep the insulation in place, so it wouldn't blow back into these great clumps of yellow crap? Probably wouldn't have worked.

Might have worked.

Wouldn't be any worse.

I can't do this, I'm going down again. I'll do it in the morning when it's cooler.

Well this has been an hour well spent! Done nothing and I'm more tired than I was when I was still outside doing the soffits. I am so fed up.

'What? I can't. You go. I'm up here – in the roof space.'

'OK, sorry. I'll come down.'

'Karen! Mary Lou! Wow!'

'Carol! It's Karen and Mary Lou'

'Oh! It's wonderful to see you! I didn't know you were coming.'

'Obviously, otherwise you'd have dressed up!'

'No, I've been in the . . . Carol, it's Karen and Mary Lou.'

'You've driven all the way from Miami? Well, yes, there is a lot to do. You've brought what with you? You are the kindest people in the world.'

And with that we went out and helped them bring in the tarps, sterno canisters, pool shock and a Christmas gift list of other things that we either need or might need. Including fruit juice.

Kindness is the greatest of all human qualities and it is here in huge proportion.

These two amazing ladies are clients of mine. And they wanted to be helpful while they go on to a rental property they own to meet with a public loss adjuster. A four hour drive here, a four hour drive back and they took this detour in case they could bring some things we might need. And because there are no phones they just guessed what to bring. And because they had no idea where we live they worked it out as best they could. Because without many road signs to look at the map isn't ever so useful – or has low current functionality to quote this dear friend from the east coast.

'I can't get over it. You drove all this way. You are ministering angels.

You're not even stopping? You have too much to do. Yes, I'm sure you have. I just can't thank you enough.'

And with that two of the cleverest, kindest people we know got back in their car and pulled out of the street.

'What fantastic friends we have!' said Carol as we stood and watched them go.

'Fantastic is right.'

And feeling so cared for I took off my gorilla suit and went back up the ladder and continued to punch staples into the heavy plastic sheeting. And thought about how very fortunate we are.

I do love living in America! People are so caring and helpful. Neighborly is the word. Everyone is just flat out neighborly. I just can't imagine going through a destructive event like a hurricane and not know that everyone is looking out for everyone else like they are doing here. If having your community destroyed has any good in it, it's that we have all remembered who we are and who our neighbors are.

And by neighbors I don't just mean everyone living close by. I mean all those good folk from outside of our county who are giving their time and effort and money to help us. Red Cross volunteers, church volunteers, Salvation Army volunteers, clubs and civic groups who are arriving every day to hand out water and ice and prepare food for those poor folk who have lost their homes completely. And I mean two ladies who have just driven from Miami.

THANK YOU!

The FEMA lady

Oh! A knock on the door. (doorbell not linked to generator; probably wouldn't hear it, anyway, with all the noise it makes).

Who's this for crying out loud? Don't they know we're watching television? Perhaps they do know and that's why they're here. Well they'd better be quiet and sit still.

So I said to Carol 'Go and see who's at the never mind I'll go.' (Well done me old shipmate, you know what happened last time you asked her to do something. We don't want to tempt the Fates and get another hurricane, now, do we?)

'Hello,' I said.

'Hello,' she said back (fair enough) 'I'm from FEMA, may I come in?'

'FEMA? Yes you most certainly may. 'Carol! It's the government', I shouted, 'and she didn't say I'm here to help you.' (Another old joke.)

So the young lady came in, sat down, got out her handheld laptop (programmed in color from the look of it) and off she jolly well went.

All round the happy home.

Roof. Click.

Ceilings. Click.

Front porch. Click.

Pool cage. Click.

Everything that Charley knocked about or took with him. Click, click, click. Does this lady from the government miss nothing? She walks, she sees, she clicks.

'Did you buy the generator because of the hurricane?'

'Yes' Click

'Did you buy a chain saw?'

'No, but I can go and get one if that would help.'

No Click

'Are you unemployed because of the hurricane?'

'I sell real estate, what do you think?'

Click Click.

Such a nice lady and judging by the accent not from these parts. And as the handheld laptop whirred we indulged in polite conversation

'Are you American citizens?' she asked.

'No,' we were quick to reply, 'we have Green Cards; we're resident aliens waiting for Uncle Sam to send us our citizenship pack so we can color it in and send it back to see if we win a prize.'

Carol told me to behave and not to joke with the government.

'Oh, that's fine,' the kind lady remarked, 'where are you from?'

'England! Land of Hope and Glory, Mother of the Free!'

'I'm from Oklahoma.'

'Wow! I always loved that musical. 'Ducks and chicks and geese better scurry' (also two legs) 'how did you get into government work after that? Do they have hurricanes in Hollywood?'

'I meant the State, not the show,' she said.

I pretended to understand what she meant and skillfully changed the subject

'So how much money can we have and does it matter if we've got insurance and does it matter if we've got some money in the bank?'

'These are your tax dollars at work' she calmly responded.

I'm brilliant at changing subjects.

And with that she left.

In a Chevy, not a surrey by the way.

'Well that was nice, wasn't it?' I said. 'I wonder if the government will send us all our taxes back. Or just some of them back would be nice.' Just enough to pay for some ear plugs.

I wonder when our insurance company will send out the loss adjuster?

Anyway, the television (oooh!) is on.

Talk to me Lois; I'm all yours.

Déjà vu all over again

Pardon?

What did you say?

JIM!

What did you just say?

Hurricane Frances is where?

Hurricane Frances is doing what?

Hurricane Frances is moving in which direction?

Hurricane Frances is how big?

As big as Texas?

Do you know how big Texas is? I've been to Texas; it's huge. Texas goes on forever and Hurricane Frances is bigger than that?

Anyway, what do you mean Hurricane Frances? Where did Hurricane Frances come from all of a sudden? Why didn't someone say the F word sooner?

Oh yeah, because we didn't have a television sooner and we don't like listening to radios.

Listening to radios requires a whole new skill set. You can't sit and stare at the radio; it makes your eyes go funny because it doesn't do anything and you get a headache. Listening to a radio in the car is different. You can drive and see things move on the windshield with that radio. Sitting in a chair and not moving and listening to a radio that doesn't move can do your head in if you're used to linking sound and movement.

There's a lot more to post-hurricane living than most people think. Why don't they teach this kind of thing in schools? If I'd learned how to sit still and not see anything move and listen to the radio I'd have known about Hurricane Frances when it was still Tropical Storm Frances or even Tropical Depression "pick-a-number". I don't know about Frances not being a depression anymore, I'm getting into a depression just thinking about another hurricane.

But! Can't afford to sit and get depressed – no sirree, Bob. Things to do!

Right!

 Action stations!

All hands on deck. We need a family conference.

Talk to the hand!

That <u>was</u> a good film, wasn't it? And it gave us a new punch line for when somebody gets in your face. 'Talk to the hand!'

I said 'Talk to the hand!'

Anyway we have to have a plan. We have to make sure we have all we need. We have to be ready to move to where we can get local television programs just in case Frances comes our way even though they think it might go to Tampa. If it's bigger than Texas I really don't think it matters if it does go to Tampa. Tampa's not that far away when you measure things in Texas terms. We might be tired and we might be fed up and we might not have much money (having given it all to the government on April 15th) but we have to be strong; it's the right thing to do.

So. What's the first thing to do? Make a list. No, "begin with the end in mind", that's what. And the end would be? – no hurricane. The *Seven Habits of Highly Effective Hurricanes* should give us all we need to make a plan. So, the end would be – be safe and sound. Us and the house, and the neighbors. Easy enough. I could delegate all that stuff to Carol and Laura while I go into the garage and sharpen the saw.

Who has "sharpening the saw" as a highly-effective habit I've no idea; sounds more like compulsive-obsessive disorder to me but everybody I know seems to have read the book (apart from me, for some reason).

Drat!

Why didn't I plan ahead and read the book? There has to be more to 'sharpening the saw' than sharpening saws.

Double Drat!

No time to solve the puzzle now. I could ask Lor but then she'd know I'd not read it. She's only just found out I can't do roofs on my own; I don't really want her to know I don't read stuff, either. I don't listen to radios, I don't read. I could borrow Jim's saw but Laura would know it wasn't mine. I could remind everybody I made electricity and say this next hurricane is theirs.

Blood and sand!

Thank you, Lois! We have a hurricane checklist. Use the checklist.

But this time do it like we mean it! It's not just having enough water to drink and not buying any pizzas (easy to cook but they go soft because the generator lacks umph, so you just throw them away.)

And, anyway, we hardly ate anything after the last one. We worked so hard that we didn't have an appetite; we just drank water and picked at bits and got in lines for free stuff and went to Venice to use their stores and telephone capability. And, anyway, cheese is much too rich when you've had a hurricane. My stomach couldn't deal with anything as rich as cheese.

So, what do we need to make sure we're safe and sound and comfortable and feel as good about things as we can? And how do we make sure we can go from "recover and restore" to "maintain"?

This time we want to be as comfortable as possible and we don't want to have to waste things we didn't use last time or go out for stuff we didn't have last time but should have had. We have to keep sharp (like the saw).

We have to use what we know and think about what we could have done better so we do it right this time.

And we have to make the right decisions at the right time.

And we have to know that this time we might lose the roof completely and that means we would have to live somewhere else – put that on the list.

OK. So where's Frances and where is she going and how quickly and why should they know more about this one than the last one?

If I learned one thing from Charley it's that nobody spells Charley that way. And the other thing I learned is that hurricanes only pretend to have a plan. And also that. . .

If I learned two things it's that hurricanes only pretend to have a plan. And the other thing is that you have to stay one step ahead and you do that by checking on it twice a day and the second time (usually at the eleven o' clock update) you decide whether you should change your plan.

So. Where is the little blighter? (big blighter)

Off the east coast.

Travelling? West-northwest.

At?

Not very fast per hour.

High pressure up at the top. Another high pressure a long, long way off to the left; too far from my favorite sticky out bit to make a difference. How high is the *High* close at hand? Will it get higher and higher or will it chicken out and move off back to Bermuda? This is the stuff of which decisions are made.

Ha! I'm not just a power house of generator manuals I am a hurricane fighter.

You gotta know when to hold and know when to fold, know when to walk away and know when to run.

And in which direction. Running the wrong way won't help.

I am definitely "up" for this one. Come on Frances; let's see what you got!

And let's see why they named you after two or more European countries.

So, our (extremely) recently updated checklist of hurricane preparedness things to do enables us to check off many things quite quickly e.g. put up hurricane shutters (still up) get water (just got back from National Guardsmen to-go place at Walgreen's) stockpile essential repair items (still have tarps, duct tape, rope from before which we didn't use). Our preparedness is exceedingly impressive. We're all still very unhappy about it, though.

Decisions, decisions

Now, then. Do we hold, fold, walk or run?

Reasons for holding? To protect our little love nest.

Reasons for folding, walking away or running? To protect life and limb.

This is why twice-daily updates are so important. If we wanted to get to safer ground, what are the options?

#1 decide where safer ground might be – answer: must be further away than Texas-sized hurricane.

#2 consider where this might be – answer: Kentucky, Virginia and everywhere else we have friends who have said at least once "drop in and say hello if you're ever in town".

When you go on vacation and you meet someone they always say "Good to meet you, really enjoyed our time together, drop in and say hello if you're ever in town"

Well now I know why they say it. I always just thought it was one of those polite things people say at the end of a vacation. But, no; it's because they know there's always the possibility of a second hurricane. People are very thoughtful.

#3 how do we get to "beyond Texas"? Answer: drive to airport and fly.

#4 which airport? Answer: all of them.

This is simple, use the old credit card to reserve a hotel room in any of all the towns close to airports within a 4 hour drive. Put a 24 hour "hold" on airline tickets from the local airport to destination of choice.

Then . . . watch for direction, strength and size of H. Frances and drive in appropriate direction remembering to cancel all unnecessary hotel rooms before 6.00pm on night of arrival and release the hold on unwanted airline tickets.

This saw is sharper than it looks.

Well it looks as though, according to my **television** that Frances isn't going to strengthen beyond your basic hurricane strength. So, life and limbs will be safe and sound. All we have to do is protect the old homestead from strong wind.

But I must say I'm not really looking forward to another day or night of that flaming noise.

However, best foot forward. What are the obvious prep jobs?

Check the list.

Then climb up on the roof (again) to double-ensure we've got enough wood strips, boards and nails to keep those tarps in place. Keep the rain out, keep the ceilings up; that's what it's all about.

Pretty simple, really.

Waiting for a hurricane when you know what hurricanes are like is rather like waiting to climb into the dentist's chair when you know what dentists are like.

And the wind begins to rise.

And it rises and rises for hours and hours. And it rains and rains for hours and hours.

Waiting for something the size of Texas to pass over is like waiting for the Death Star in Star Wars to pass over. You know it's big, you know it's dangerous, you know it holds your life in its hands but you don't know if it's going to do anything about it. But, boy oh boy, does it take a long time.

Texas is very big and very slow moving. But, we seemed to do alright.

Interestingly we didn't need to climb back in the closet. Big and slow as dear old Frances was by the time her Texas-sized bulk got to us she had pretty much run out of puff. Hurricane Frances was just plain old Tropical Storm Frances. And no more frightening than my elementary school principal who, at the time, seemed fairly scary but in hindsight dear old Mrs. Evans wasn't frightening at all. She just seemed to get in the way and stop me from playing – rather like Tropical Storm Frances! Except Frances didn't last as long as my elementary school career. And from what I remember I also graduated that with a fail. But no one remembers and no one cares – sic Gloria transit!

(Gloria is Latin, not a new hurricane so you can all relax.)

The last of the solar panels certainly banged around a lot while she did last (Frances, not Gloria). Noise, noise, noise, noise, noise. Bang, bang, bang, bang, bang (wind). Swish, swish, swish, swish, swish (rain)

Time to check to see whether we held.

'Oh good', said Carol (of television fame) 'the ceiling's got damp patches on it.'

'Well, when the solar panels come off they probably take the holding screws with them and they leave holes big enough for the water to get through. So you see, the water runs down the joists and spreads out across the ceiling. And that's why it's damp.' I said without thinking, and without considering the consequences of attempting to instruct my wife at a time when instruction was probably a little unnecessary.

'Stuff it!' she responded.

'You probably already knew that, didn't you?'

I said 'Stuff it'.

'You did'.

'So stuff it, then'

'Yes'

And we didn't talk about it anymore!

But we were very happy that we could relax and not have to clench our jaws and look up at the ceiling all the time. Not that we relaxed but we weren't as tense.

'Cup of tea?'

'Yes, please!'

'You see what Jim and Lois have got to say and I'll get another tarp and go up on the roof.' (Purely by way of a change.)

Even when they are named after two or more European countries, second hurricanes can be rather draining – even when they are really only tropical storms.

The rain and the damp patches on the ceiling were real enough.

I really am tired of climbing up ladders and standing on hot, steep, scary roofs. But at least now I know how to. I wonder if it will help to think of Hurricane Charley as mere practice for Hurricane Frances?

I've just tried it and it doesn't help.

'Good grief, those solar panel screw holes are big!' I thought as I looked at the side where they'd been.

It's strange what you think about when you're up on a roof.

If our loss adjuster had come yesterday this repair would have been an after-the-fact repair and so subject to a second deductible on the old insurance policy.

'I wonder if we can keep him away until after the third hurricane?' I mumbled to myself.

'Give over, Tony, there isn't going to be a third hurricane! Just push some silicon in the holes and nail down another tarp.'

Blood and sand but I'm tired.

Lights, Ivan, action

'What are you going on about?'

'Just what are you going on about?'

I just asked you a question, Jim.

WHAT

ARE

YOU

GOING

ON ABOUT?

WHAT?

I just don't believe this. Hurricane Ivan is in the Caribbean. Jim, come on! Don't do this, Jim! Put Lois on.

Hurricane Ivan!

Hurricane Ivan had better stay in the flaming Caribbean,

'Stay in the Caribbean, Ivan! In fact you can go right back to the Azores and sit out in the middle of the Atlantic and leave me alone!'

Hurricane Ivan! How do I tell my family there's another hurricane on its way? For crying out loud, I think I've had enough.

I'm tired and fed up and I don't want another hurricane.

Or another tropical storm.

Or even another cloud with a strong breeze.

I just want to sit and be still and moan about television programs and getting another puncture because of all the stupid nails that drop off the backs of trucks hauling debris to the landfills.

My idea of a good time right now is to moan about being bored and having to watch the same old television programs and be hot and sweaty. Is that too much to ask? I just want to stand in line and get bottled water. I just want to wait for the Red Cross lady to come round with the plastic dinners. I just want to fix another puncture.

I do not want another hurricane!

I already know how this one will go. They'll call it *Ivan the Terrible*.

It's a little obvious but that's what they'll do. Some joker on one of the weather forecasts will laugh a little and say "Now let's check on Ivan the Terrible." And that'll be it; it will be Ivan the Terrible from then on.

Ivan the Terrible's a stupid name. Ivan the Russian Tsar (which for some reason they spell Czar, as though he was Czechoslovak or something) wasn't even called *Terrible* he was called *Dread*. John the Dread was his name and title. Ivan Grozny. "Never was a king more loved nor more feared" if I remember my history studies correctly.

And I'll tell you this; Hurricane Ivan might well be feared but there's no way on earth he will be loved. Not by anybody. Not by me, not by my family, not by our neighbors, not even by chief meteorologists who wouldn't have anything to say without him.

Hurricane Ivan is bad news.

But the good news is a Florida Power and Light truck drove very slowly along our street looking at every pole and every transformer. They've been shipping in truck load after truck load of poles and cable. The interstate, more or less, has a "truck lane" I didn't really know what a convoy was until now. Dozens and dozens, hundreds and hundreds of trucks, line after line, bumper to bumper, mile after mile, day after day. These guys just keep coming. We see them on our Venice runs when we go to get groceries and make phone calls.

We knew the guys were working in our subdivision; been here for days. Closed off one of the main feeder roads – just closed it off; no access, no how, no way. Putting utility poles in takes a lot of time and a lot of heavy equipment. And a lot of road space, of course. So they close off whole sections of the subdivision. And now we wait with baited breath.

'Check all the light switches,' said Carol.

'Pardon?' I responded as niftily as I could, trying to avoid another obvious comment

'They don't work; we haven't got any power.'

'I know,' she said. 'But if they're checking on our street maybe we're going to get power. If everything's switched on there might be a surge and blow something, so check everything and switch everything off – except for one light. If it comes on we'll have power and we can add things slowly.'

'You're brilliant.' I said.

'No, just a woman.'

Maybe all women are born great and I'd just not noticed.

I wonder if we'll miss being hot and sticky and lining up for ice when we get silent electricity.

It's very quiet waiting for electricity. (Except for the generator.) No one speaks. You just sit and watch the light bulb. (And listen to the generator.)

Sit and watch the light bulb.

Sit and watch the light bulb.

'YES!'

Hugs and kisses.

'Go and tell Shirl in case she doesn't know. Tell Frank and Nancy. Tell everybody.'

'You tell them, I'm turning off that bl**dy generator.'

'Just a minute! Air conditioning! We can have air!'

'Switch on the air conditioning; see if it comes on.' Carol seemed to be almost whispering. Like she was balancing on a beam that was hanging over a cliff – you know, speak too loudly and the beam goes off balance and you fall. It was as if we could blow the A/C unit just by talking too loudly.

So I very gingerly moved the little lever from *off* to *auto*.

3 seconds. 5 seconds. 7 seconds. It seemed like an hour.

And it worked! We have air conditioning. You can live without air conditioning but you can't live without television, it seems.

Now we have both.

It was one of those "Lights. Camera. Action." moments. We have electricity. We have air conditioning. The world is getting back to normal for our little family down at the bottom of the sticky-out bit.

'And the freezer can make ice!'

'I know.'

And no more late night trips to the loo by flashlight. Life just don't get any better than this.

Yes it does – life without Ivan would be better.

We sat for a few minutes, relaxing, and being quiet. I looked out of the window as best I could – through the gap in the middle where I'd taken out a couple of the storm panels. I looked over at Carol. I could see she was thinking about something. She wasn't relaxed or "deep in thought" she was just, obviously, thinking about something.

Ivan, argument, sadness

'I want to leave,' said Carol in a voice that was something between emphatic and fragile.

'I know you do, me Darlin', but we don't know enough to be able to make that decision.'

'I just want to leave. I can't stand another hurricane.'

'I know. And I don't want another hurricane, either, but we can't just up and go.'

'Why not?'

'Because we don't know what this hurricane will do. We don't know where it will go. We don't know where to leave to or when to leave. We can't just *go*.'

'I want to.'

'Well if you really want to, book a flight and I'll take you to the airport. Go to Kentucky and stay with Chris and John.'

'I want you to come, too.'

'I'm not leaving until I know more. Just making an off-the-cuff decision to leave isn't sensible.'

'I'm afraid.'

'I'm afraid, too, but as I said with Frances, the reason for leaving is to save our lives; the reason for staying is to save our home.'

'The home is only a thing. If we die it won't matter whether the home is here or not!'

I went and sat beside her, my dear wife, my heroine, my worried, sad, tired, frightened, wonderful heroine. And I put her hand in mine.

'I know the house is only a thing' I said, 'but it is our home and the threat of dying, well, that's an extreme case. The chances are that we won't get hit. If we do it's likely to be a Category 1 or Category 2 storm. That won't kill us but it might kill the tarps and if we're three days away we lose the home. That's not something I'm prepared to do. In a few days we'll know the situation and we can decide then what to do.'

'By then it will be too late. The airports will be closed and the roads will be parking lots.'

'It won't be too late. And unless we decide to leave Florida we don't know where to go to. Remember Charley; look at how many people evacuated to Orlando and then had to evacuate again. Making a panic decision doesn't keep us safe; it could put us in exactly the wrong place.'

'I want to leave!'

'I'll take you to the airport.'

'That's not what I mean and you know it!'

'I'm not leaving until I know I should leave and until I know where to leave to.'

'I want to leave! I want to leave, you stupid, selfish man!'

'I'm not going!'

And suddenly the air conditioning and the fans and the prospect of ice from the refrigerator and no generator noise lost a lot of meaning.

Now it was time to be angry with each other and to feel hurt and to be quiet. Now it was how it is when you've nothing to do but wonder about what to do. Watch the Weather Channel, check the

NOAA web site, worry about what might happen in the next few days, avoid eye contact.

And it was time to feel embarrassed and to wonder about what if I'm wrong.

Blood and sand, but I'm fed up!

And how selfish is that? I'm fed up with air conditioning and an ice dispenser. All those poor souls who lost their homes to Charley suffered through Frances and now face the prospect of losing their trailers and PODS to Ivan. What have I got to be fed up about?

After about an hour I said

'I'm sorry; I don't mean to upset you.'

'I know.'

'Let's talk about what we should do.'

'We should leave.'

'That's not the answer. We can't just leave.

What about Shirley and Jim? What about Nancy and Frank?

We can't just up and off to nowhere in particular.

If we get hit with a Category 1 storm and lose our tarps the water will destroy our home.

We can't expect our neighbors to come to our rescue. Good grief, Carol, I'm the one who's been climbing on other people's roofs putting up tarps for them. Who can do ours if they're damaged?'

'If Jim and Shirley want to evacuate will you take us?'

'Of course I will, if it's necessary; I just won't go today or tomorrow. We'll not be any less worried 200 or 500 miles away. And if the *High* stays where it is Ivan will stay out in the Gulf.'

'You said that about Charley. "Oh we never get hurricanes; we're protected by the Bermuda High and the continental cold front" 'that's what you said but you were wrong. And then we got Frances. Another hurricane we weren't supposed to get. And now it's Ivan.'

And then she shouted.

'Why can't you just admit you know nothing about hurricanes? You're ignorant and stupid and selfish! Just

admit it, will you?'

'Yes I know I was wrong and I know there's a lot I don't know about hurricanes. But there's also a lot I do know. The Bermuda High moved and the cold front didn't come as far south as it usually does. But that doesn't mean it won't hold this time. For years the high pressure has protected this part of Florida and for the next few days it should continue to protect us.'

'Shut up! I'm not listening! Shut up!'

Silence.

And awkwardness.

And sadness.

That is how it is in our house just now.

I feel sick. I hate this life. Nothing happened for ten minutes or something like that.

I just sat.

Carol just sat.

We both just sat.

'And what if it doesn't?' She asked

'What if what doesn't?'

'What if the High doesn't hold?'

'By then we'll know where the hurricane is and where it will probably go and how strong it is.'

'We didn't know that for Charley.'

'Yes we did – well we knew where it was and where it was likely to make landfall. We didn't know its strength until it was too late, but to be honest, being one degree out in a forecast landfall is really a bullseye when you're talking about something as big and unstable as a hurricane.'

'Oh shut up!'

'No, you must listen to me, that's all I ask – just listen, don't judge. The strength for Charley was wrong and I'm convinced it was because the pressure monitors failed, not because it went from a

Category 2 to a 4 inside half an hour. Hurricanes can't generate that much energy in half an hour. Something was wrong; they won't be wrong again. And if they weren't wrong the data didn't come in quickly enough'

'You don't know that!'

'No, I don't but I'm as sure as I can be. We knew the *High* was weakening, days before Charley hit. We knew Charley would make landfall close to us.

When they said Tampa to Naples they were dead right; we're midway between Tampa and Naples. What no one knew was how strong it was. Hurricane Ivan will not take us by surprise. Everyone is monitoring pressure gradients and the storm and who knows what else. They'll tell us things days beforehand and if it looks like our lives will be in danger we will go and we'll take whoever we can with us. But if our lives are not in danger I'm not going to lose our home to rains and floods just because we got emotional and didn't use our brains.'

'I want to think about it.'

'We'll both think about it and we'll both decide – all of us, that is – you, me, Lor.'

'Make me a drink.'

'OK.'

Ivan and the Navy

Hurricane Ivan is a MONSTER.

The *Bermuda High* is holding.

If it continues to hold, Ivan will stay in The Gulf. Those poor souls in the Panhandle. They've been hit every year for the past three or four years and this will be a big one. It's so wrong to feel relieved knowing someone else will suffer. If Ivan blew itself out in The Gulf we'd just feel relieved; relieved and happy. As it is we feel relieved and guilty. We can't stop Ivan from doing what it's going to do.

What's that saying? *The wind god blows where the wind god chooses.*

Which isn't true, of course. The Caribs and the Maya didn't know about the *Bermuda High*. They just knew that nothing could stop Huracan.

Huracan the wind god, the bringer of storms and flood and fire. Huracan the creator and the destroyer. Huracan created the land and also caused the great flood. If Huracan blew his great breath he caused devastation; if he passed by he spared the villages.

The wind god blows where the wind god chooses is a fatalistic yet strangely comforting viewpoint. Today we know that Huracan is not all-powerful; he is the vassal of the Bermuda High. Hurican cannot move the High and he cannot burst through the High. He must skirt the edge of the High. He seeks permission from a greater power to blow where he is allowed. Huracan goes where the jet stream chooses and where the continental cold front chooses and where the Bermuda High chooses.

Huracan takes the line of least resistance.

But, Blood and sand, you know he's there. And those poor folk up in the Panhandle are going to know in full measure just how powerful a hurricane it is.

And so is our loss adjuster.

The man from the insurance company has cancelled again.

"Hello, I'm your insurance loss adjuster. I'd like to come and see you."

"Oops! Can't come; Hurricane Frances is coming. I'm going to evacuate."

"Hello. I'm your insurance loss adjuster. I'd like to come and see you."

"Oops! Can't come; Hurricane Ivan is coming. I'm going to evacuate."

"Hello, I'm your new insurance loss adjuster. The other loss adjuster lives in Louisiana. He's not coming back to Florida. He is going to stay with his family." Poor chap. He spends his life sorting out other people's hurricane losses and now he's going through his own.

So, our very own loss adjuster cometh. Well, almost. Mr. Matt is also being evacuated but at least he's promising to return. He lives in Texas. I wonder if he knows that Texas is about the same size as Hurricane Frances? I wonder if the Bermuda High will hold?

'I'm still frightened!'

'I know you are, me Darlin'. I'm frightened, too, but the High is holding firm. Ivan will not come all that close to us.'

'What if the High doesn't hold and it moves off like it did before?'

'It moved off days before, not one day before. That's why we got hit. The High weakened and moved away. Look at NOAA, look at what NOAA is saying. It's obvious we'll be OK.'

'Look at NOAA!' She hissed, 'What do they know that all the other forecasters don't know?'

'Listen to me! Please! NOAA is a Navy system. The Navy uses more real-time readings than any other forecasting system. NOAA has more ships and more buoys and it relies on them for up to the minute readings. All that raw data goes into actual mapping and graphs. Some other forecasters use NOAA to feed into their computer models. NOAA is real, most of the others are models made up of lots of data – current, real-time data and past, merged data.

Too much data in my opinion. And the other real-time forecasters use fewer "at sea" stations for their readings. NOAA is safer than the others – and their "forecasting balloon" makes more sense than the "cone of uncertainty" other forecasters tell us about. And for all I like Jim and Lois, Robert Van Winkle is an ex-Navy guy. He used to be a meteorologist on the Nimitz. He is the most accurate as far as I'm concerned. Ivan will miss us. We won't even get tropical storm winds.

If we lived in the Panhandle I would come here. I'm telling you, me Darlin', Ivan will wreak devastation up through Georgia, Virginia, and maybe right up in Kentucky. Maybe even New

England. The only place that's safer than where we are right now is flaming Miami.'

'Are you certain?'

'I'm as certain as I can be. This is a safe place this time.'

'All right, we'll stay. But you'd better be right'

The loss adjuster

There are two things about me which I've always liked:–

#1 I'm married to Carol.

#2 I have a Marvin Rainwater record. (Only kidding about #2)

#2 is that I am actually quite good at understanding things and making reasonably good decisions. And I know this decision is the right one. Staying here is the right thing to do.

And Hurricane Ivan did just what I thought he would do – miss us by miles and, unfortunately, plow right into the Panhandle.

Hurricane Ivan destroyed so much of other people's lives and homes. We felt relieved and guilty. Which, on balance, is better than feeling violated which is how hurricanes make you feel.

They bulldoze their way into your life, they destroy and steal and hurt.

They tire you out and leave behind sadness and pain which doesn't go away because there's always something to remind you that you were violated.

Anyway! Mr. Matt, the loss adjuster, has returned and wants to come and play.

Ding dong ding said the front door – as front doors do when you have proper electricity.

'Hi! I'm Matt from . . .' said this very cheerful young man

'Hi! I'm Tony from here.' I blurted out before he could finish his sentence

'Stop messing about.' Came the sweet voice from in front of the television.

'I can!' He's not from the government. I saw his car.'

'Forgive my husband; he's quite bright and nearly house-trained but sometimes he gets to the door before I do.'

'No problem' said Mr. Matt. I think Matt will be my friend.

'May I take a look around?' He said

'Of course; sorry the place is a bit of a mess; we had a hurricane.'

'Tony!'

'I'm just saying.'

'Get the paperwork ready so we can have a sensible conversation about what needs to be done.'

I got the paperwork and laid it out on the table. Matt returned; he had a hand held computer just like the FEMA lady. And he walked and looked and clicked. Just like the FEMA lady.

'You have a list of items?' He queried.

'Serpently do.' I responded.

'Good, let's take a look and compare notes.'

I must say that I've always been a fan of my insurance company; they've always been very fair and seem to know about that thing called "customer care". And today was going to be no exception.

'You need a new roof, you know that don't you?'

'Yes and we could have had one before Frances came but your head office said no permanent repairs until the adjuster's been.'

'Rules is rules.' Said Mr. Matt

Well I have to say old Mr. Matt had a longer list than I had but then he is the expert and probably just saw more stuff than I did.

'Who cleaned out your pool?' He said

'I did' said Carol

'And who erected the safety fence?'

'I did' said Carol

'Well it needed a screwdriver.' I was quick to comment. 'And I'm more planning and design than operations, if you see what I mean. And cleaning pools is a bit like housework.'

Mr. Matt looked like something between stunned and embarrassed.

'Ignore him' said my better half. 'I did the pool; Brainiac, here, did the roof and heavy lifting. And the trees and the neighbors' roofs and if we'd had proper electricity he'd also have done the ironing. He just likes to make housework jokes.'

'Good' said a relieved looking loss adjuster who was, again, looking like he knew where to put himself.

'Well the pool work is claimable, so I'll add $600 to the amount, shall I?'

'$600? $600 for the pool? What about something for the roof?'

'Sorry, roof work doesn't count. You can claim for the tarps, though, and all the other incidentals. Roof work isn't like housework, you see.'

'Ouch! Hoist by my own petard.' I mumbled to myself

'There's a moral, there, Sunshine!' came the sweet voice of reason from behind my ear.

So, Mr. Matt checked his list with our list and came up with a large amount of money. We showed him the estimates we'd been able to get. And the bills for the repair materials. And we told him we'd chosen well-established contractors we knew. He seemed satisfied we'd done it right and he said we didn't need to get lots of estimates and that when we do get estimates for the work we'd not been able to so far we just needed to call him. He could give us a verbal approval and the paperwork could follow.

Mr. Matt is a good guy. He trusted our judgment on estimates and choice of contractors and as long as we keep going he'll make life a little easier for us. Getting three estimates for each job is just about impossible, anyway. And since we're not going to get a general contractor to handle everything that should keep our total claim down. Even though I'm not much good with screwdrivers, myself, I do know how they **should** be used and we know enough good contractors who will do a good job to be confident that our home and the insurer's bank account will come out just fine.

It's amazing how good we feel just having had a meeting with an insurance chap. We actually feel we are getting somewhere.

And not feeling helpless is wonderful.

So now I can get to work sorting the contractors and checking that what they said is what they'll do and then making sure they do it.

In fact I'm feeling so wonderful I'm almost "up" for a game of Monopoly. But I know what I will do; I'll take my car down to the emergency claims car center and see what they think of all those dents, dings, scratches and marks left by Hurricane Charley, Hurricane Frances and Hurricane Ivan.

The car claim

It's very hot in an emergency-claims damaged-vehicle tent. But they do provide cold drinks.

I don't like "car" places. One of the nicest people I've ever met used to own a car dealership but I'm just not good in car places. Buying cars is always unpleasant for me. I know that no matter what, I'm going to get rolled over. I don't know if that's true, it's probably not true but it just feels like it's true and so I avoid "car" places. Buying a new anything is usually pleasant but buying a new car is not. Not for me.

This car place, however, is like no other – it's a tent, it's in a supermarket parking lot. There aren't any salesmen with reflective sunglasses and the only person to smile at me was the young lady who registered me and gave me a bottle of water.

So I sit

And sit

And sit

And sit.

This is how Edmond Dantés felt in *The Count of Monte Cristo* –

except I know I will escape. And it won't take seventeen years. (Sorry; if you've not read *The Count of Monte Cristo* I didn't mean to spoil it – and anyway, that's not how it ends.) It's a fantastic story written by Alexandre Dumas (pronounced Doomah, not dumbass) which everyone should read.

So, anyway, a very pleasant young man has just taken my car keys. He and another young man are looking at every scratch and ding and dent and glass crack and dirty mark and they're pointing to things and writing stuff down and making check marks and going round again and

'Pardon? There's how much damage? $5,500 worth? Are you sure? You're not just saying that because I'm feeling out of place and I don't like car showrooms?'

'Pardon? And you're cutting the check, now?' I think I'm in love.

And after a few more minutes I'm given a check with my name on it for five thousand five hundred dollars. We can live for a good few weeks on $5,500. I don't have to book the car in just yet and I don't have to drive to Sarasota to have it counter-signed by the mortgage guy. This is my money and I've got it now.

'Thank you.' I said in a very positive way. 'Take care, guys. I really appreciate it.'

And with that I walked away towards my car.

It has the damage and I have the five and a half grand. That's five thousand five hundred dollars. Five thousand five hundred dollars (say it soft and it's almost like five thousand six hundred dollars!)

But I didn't quite make it.

'Pardon?

You made a mistake?'

Well wouldn't you know! That's car places for you! The Lord giveth and the Lord taketh away – or in this case a rotten, stinking, lousy insurance guy.

'Yeah. Of course. Here's the check back.'

'Yeah, I'll sit over here, again.'

Well, nice while it lasted. For a few minutes I was cock o' the walk. Five and a half grand for mortgage payments and car payments and electricity bills and gas money and food. Five and a half grand that I didn't have take out of my savings account. Well at least no one knows but me. No one else relaxed for a few minutes feeling good about life. Carol's probably just wondering if I got another puncture or how long it'll take me before I get back to continue with the workload.

Yeah. It's just me who's feeling racked off.

'Pardon? It's not enough? You forgot to add $500 for car hire while mine's in the shop being repainted? And that's the maximum allowed in my policy? And you're sorry? Don't be sorry, sir, you take your time.'

'Are you kidding me?' I thought to myself. I'm walking away with five and a half grand and they want to give me more.

This is the best insurance company in the world. I tell you, this is a lot better than picking the Chance card – Bank error in your favor; collect $200. This is $500 and it's real and I won't have to give it back when I land on a green one.

Life is getting back on track!

And what's that? That pharmacy is giving away palettes of bottled water? I'm going in. I must admit to feeling rather guilty. It's a funny feeling. My home is totally "livable", the insurance guy is approving our repair work, both our cars are fully drivable and I've just been given about three months' living expenses and now I'm picking up free water.

It's a strange feeling.

So many folk have lost everything, they've even lost the boxes they were semi-living in.

You see them walking around still looking in a daze.

You see them lining up for free food looking as though they'll cry at any moment, they walk so slowly and I've got all this money and a home and two cars and more water. I have a right to it but I feel guilty.

Laura's roof is gone, she can't go home, she spends all day helping clients work through their traumas and their lack of insurance cover and their lack of income because where they worked has been destroyed. And she never complains about being tired or having to work such long hours. She doesn't even talk about it, she just comes home and sits and gets ready for bed and gets up and goes out, again.

It'll be a long time before we're really back on track.

Thinking about Jeanne

Jeanne, Jeanne, Bonnie Jeanne.

Jeanne is not Bonnie. Jeanne is going to be a little half-hitch, if you know Cockney slang.

Jeanne. Hurricane Jeanne.

Hurricane Jeanne.

Well at least we don't have to make any preparations.

Hurricane Jeanne! Are you flaming kidding me?

I really am tired of hurricanes and storms and being worried and being tired and being apprehensive. I'm just fatigued, I suppose.

Fatigued! *Fatigued* always sounds worse than *tired*. Metal doesn't get tired, metal suffers from fatigue. And that's just how I feel. I was strong and now I'm fatigued. And guilty, of course; I feel guilty for feeling so fatigued.

I know there are people who do have so much more to bear than I do. There are people who don't know what a good meal is, who have never drunk clean water, who live in shanty towns or war zones or have walked hundreds of miles to a refugee camp, just to avoid being tortured or killed. So I do feel guilty. Guilty and fatigued.

I think of my granddad who walked across Europe as a sixteen-year-old to escape the tyranny of an empire, and who never saw any of his family again. And all I've got to worry about is Hurricane

Jeanne. So as well as feeling tired I'm feeling guilty.

Change the subject.

As my old buddy, Geoff, would say – *Think beautiful thoughts and the world is a beautiful place.*

What could be beautiful about Hurricane Jeanne?

The name, of course!

The name.

Jeanne, Jeanne, Bonnie Jeanne.

Bonnie comes from the French for "good".

There are a lot of French words used in Scotland. The Scots and the French were always on each other's side fighting the English. Portugal is England's oldest ally; France is Scotland's old ally. And lots of French words became Scottish words, as a result of that.

"Bonnie" being one of them.

And "marmalade". And "Braw".

But not "Sassenach", that's pure Gaelic. Scots call Englishmen "Sassenachs". It means "Saxons".

I'm a Sassenach to your average Scotsman. Funny, really, because I'm Irish-Latvian; but not a lot of people know that, as Michael Cane would say. Not a lot of Saxon blood courses through my veins. My great-great-grandfather was English and that's pretty much it.

Anyway, back to Jeanne – the little half-hitch. Cockney slang, that's what I was thinking about.

Cockneys have their own language. They use terms and phrases, instead of ordinary words, which rhyme with the ordinary words so if you know Cockney slang you can keep up; if not, you are ell oh ess tee (lost)

Cockneys don't wear hats they wear *titfors* (tit for tat – hat). They're never alone they are always on their *todd* (Todd Sloan – rhymes with own – was a highwayman, hanged at Tyburn)

Cockney's a funny word, as well. It's Middle English. From Chaucer's day. It means "a cock's egg". Because cocks don't lay eggs, so a cock's egg is a most peculiar thing. And in 14th century England a city-dweller was a most peculiar thing, so they were known as cock's eggs (or cockneys). And the only place it stuck was in east London – where Cockneys now live, so there's a coincidence! Born within the sound of Bow bell. The great bell of Bow. The parish church of St Mary le Bow.

I like words. When I've got nothing to do I do words. And right now I've got nothing to do because I've done it. I'm fully prepared. Fatigued but prepared.

The only Cockney slang to have come over to the States, as far as I know, is *dukes*.

"Put up your dukes, sir." Funny, really, because to a Cockney "dukes" is fingers, not fists. (Duke of Yorks – forks). Forks is fingers. But because Cockneys never speak the rhyming bit dukes changed its meaning when it came across the pond. Imagine having a fight with someone and saying "put up your fingers."

Washington is another word I like. And Lincoln.

So many people's last names are based on places they came from. So one of George Washington's ancestors probably came from Washington – in County Durham, where I was born as it happens. (It's in Cleveland, now, because one of the English governments changed all the counties around for some reason) Cleveland in Anglo-Saxon means "hilly place" and Durham means "island with a hill" (because it's in a big bend of the river, so it looks like an island. And Durham Cathedral is at the top of a very steep hill).

Anyway, Washington is a little town that goes all the way back to Anglo-Saxon times. It means "The Place Where Wassa's People Live" – "Wassa Ing Ton". The Angles settled mainly in the centre and north of the country; the Saxons settled in the south which is why we have southern counties called Sussex and Essex and such. Lincoln is also one of my favorite words, and "acre". I like "acre". It's the original word for "land" and now means a specific amount of land.

Anyway, back to Lincoln. It predates Anglo-Saxon. It's part British and part Latin. Before the Angles and Saxons (and Jutes) came, the

Celts lived there. Some Celts spoke Gaelic (like the Picts and Scots and Irish) and some spoke Brythonic – which is how we get the word "Briton".

Anyway, in 54BC Julius Caesar (of William Shakespeare fame) invaded what he called Albion (now jolly old England) and uttered those famous words "Veni Vidi Vici". (I came, I saw, I conquered). Interestingly he also invaded the year before and got his rear end kicked by the British tribes but there is no reference to his saying "Veni Vidi and got my rear end kicked, so ran away". History only records what victors say, apparently.

So old Julius is sitting round his camp fire in 54BC, going "Am I good or what?" and then it dawned on him. No one has ever been this far west before.

(Apart from the folk who already lived there, but victors always seem to miss that point). We are actually at the edge of the world. We could fall off; anything could happen.

"I'd better secure the border", he thought.

So he got all his legionnaires in a huddle (probably) and said "Alright lads, so far so good. But what if those pesky Brits mount a counter-offensive? I have no intention of going down in history as the guy who got beat twice; we are not the Boston Red Socks, we are Romans. So I need a volunteer!"

"You! Come here."

"Who me?"

"Yes, you."

"What?"

"I've got a job for you"

"What job?"

"You are going to like this – not a lot, but you'll like it. I want you to take your legion and go as far north as you can go. And when you get there, stop. And that will be the edge of the civilized world, the final frontier, as it were, of the Roman Empire. You will be famous."

"Are you sure?"

"Yes."

"OK"

So the next morning this still-to-become-famous legionnaire took his legion and marched north.

And marched north.

And marched north.

And then it dawned on him.

"If where ever we stop is the edge of the civilized world, we can stop where ever we like. No one will ever come and check. Not even Julius Caesar".

(Oh! in case you are studying ancient history for your SAT thingies I just made that bit up. But it sounds right, doesn't it?).

So they marched until they found what I imagine to have been a rather beautiful little village in a fertile plain with lots of trees and fishing and hunting and where the natives looked friendly and they said

"Where are we?"

And the British chap they spoke with said "Llyn"

(Which was British for "lake". It wasn't a real lake, it was a big wide bit of the river but it looked like a lake, so they called it "lake") And the still-to-be-famous legionnaire said "Do you mind if we camp out a bit?"

And the friendly British tribesman said "No. We don't get many visitors, so make yourselves at home."

And the Roman legionnaire said "This will be our legionary outpost."

And the Latin for *legionary outpost* was *colonii* and so the Romans called it Llyn Colonii. And it is now known as Lincoln. So the wonderful Mr. Lincoln has a name which is composed of a place name based on two different languages. And that's why I like it so much, because it's based on two different languages, neither of which is spoken anymore but now live forever in the name of

Abraham Lincoln.

Oh yes. Jeanne. I'd forgotten about Jeanne. Hurricane Jeanne. I tend to drift off into my own thoughts.

I looked at Carol and she shrugged her shoulders at me. And I knew that that meant

'I want to leave but there's no point discussing it.'

I looked at Laura who gave me one of those kindly and understanding smiles. She understands that her mum wants to leave and that I want to stay. She understands that we're both worn down by it all. And she's kind.

I also know she would like to go home to her condo. But she can't because we have friends who completely lost their house to Charley and so they are camping out in the two rooms of her condo which are livable. So she can't even get in to her own home to try to sort it out a bit for herself. It was kind of her to put those friends before her own desire to live in her own home. She let them move in and she stayed with us.

So as well as her own thoughts and feelings our dear daughter lives through all the thoughts and feelings of her clients and, on top of that, she has to live through the thoughts and feelings of her parents as well.

Perhaps Hurricane Jeanne won't be as bad as we fear.

Party time

One of the things I like about Jim and Shirley is that when there's nothing happening they party. They are party people.

'There's nothing happening.' Said Shirl. 'Jeanne is just a bit of wind, so let's all get together and have a party.'

'It's been eight hours, Shirl' I said.

'Yeah, eight hours of some wind. When we lived in the U.P. we had days of wind; days of snow. I remember when the snow was over the roof. We didn't see daylight for weeks, the snow was so heavy. We've had eighteen feet of snow; eight hours of wind is nothing. Are you coming round or not?'

'Of course we're coming round.'

Good old Shirl.

So, in the middle of what was called Hurricane Jeanne we went across the road to Jim and Shirley's. Frank and Nancy came, so did Roger and Amy. And Jeanne blew.

And blew.

And blew.

And we drank.

And drank.

Some of us drank sodas and coffee. Jim has Scottish ancestry, so he drank what all good Scotsmen drink.

Well, after about half an hour of drinking and sharing stories and saying "Isn't it windy?" someone suggested a game of Monopoly.

'I'm leaving.' I said.

'Oh, so now he wants to leave! Where will you be leaving to?' Asked my better half, with that wry smile of hers, 'East coast? Orlando? Kentucky to be with Chris and John?

Sarcasm is what I do; I don't really expect to be on the receiving end.

'No', I said, 'just home.'

'Don't you like Monopoly, Tony?'

'No.'

'Why not?'

'It's a long story.'

'Oh do tell!'

'Well…'

'No, don't tell,' commented my dear wife, 'it's because he never wins. That's all there is to it.'

'Well it's not that I *never* win, it's . . .'

'It's because he's not won in living memory. Anyway why don't we just talk with each other? All we've done for weeks is work and arrange who's going where to get what and really do nothing more than hug each other, occasionally, and check we're all OK. Let's just be. These few minutes have been lovely, sitting together.'

'Yes, let's.' said Shirl, 'Let's visit for a while.'

And the talk continued about hurricanes and flooding and the evacuation shelter in Arcadia which lost its roof and our EMS station which lost its roof and the Emergency Operations Center which lost its roof. And someone wondered what Wayne Sallade was doing at this moment and a huge cheer went up! Wayne Sallade is our Emergency Ops Manager. For seventeen years he and his team planned and planned for when we got hit with a hurricane. And, boy, did we get hit this year? And Wayne Sallade came up trumps. I think if he stood for President he'd get every vote in this county. And Clear Channel Radio lost its roof. And the general manager had his team back on the air in four hours.

'Do you remember the first time you turned on the radio after Charley?' asked Frank, 'what did you think?'

'I was shocked,' said Shirley, 'and then felt warm. I thought if those guys can keep going, we can all keep going. It was as if they were telling us "We can do this!" I think they should get a medal. And they kept telling us where to go for supplies and which location had this and which one had that. And everything else that was happening. And which storm was coming next.'

'Don't remind me', I said, 'I remember finding out about Frances – from the TV; our radio was on its last legs, so we didn't listen to it, much. But you're right, those guys hit it out of the park for us.'

'I've been thinking,' said Roger, 'do you get hurricanes in England?'

'Yes' said my ever-loving 'and guess what Brainiac did when . . .'

'Actually, no, we don't get hurricanes in England.' I interrupted.

'Yes we do. What about Michael Fish?'

'Ah!' I replied trying to look as "in control" as I could – so I could at least try to capitalize on my victory over not playing Monopoly.

'Let me explain. You see a hurricane is a tropical weather system and is measured on the Saffir-Simpson Scale. What Great Britain gets is gales, measured on the Beaufort Scale.'

'How do you put up with him, Carol?' Asked a very sympathetic Nancy.

'Well I mainly just turn up the TV volume and pretend I'm alone.'

'No, this is important', I said in self defense, 'the storm of 1987 had hurricane force winds but it was a gale.'

'How many trees did it knock down?'

'About 15 million'.

'How strong was the wind?'

'Close to 120'.

'Well it was hurricane.'

'Alright it was a hurricane. But it was still a gale. The interesting thing, though, is that about three hours before the storm made landfall, and I happen to remember this, I was listening to the weather forecast on BBC. And the chap doing it had a drawing of a big swirly thing in the Bay of Biscay and he said "We believe it's going to be very breezy up in the Channel."

London got hit with winds gusting at Category 3 and the BBC said "very breezy". Category 3 wind speeds and they go "very breezy". The whole of London is blacked out. And it was "very breezy". To some people "very breezy" means don't take an umbrella, doesn't it? What does "very breezy" mean to you? And I love this bit; on another occasion they were talking about the Met Office tracking station and he'd just received some graphical updates and he says "Looking at the charts, it's quite magical."

'No!'

'Yes, he actually said "magical". Some things stick in your memory. A wonderful thing about meteorologists – English and American – is they really love the weather; they don't just report it, they get a thrill out of it.

But going back to Michael Fish who, incidentally, was once voted both the best-dressed and worst-dressed man on television. He was doing the weather on October 15th. It was the day before the gale (it hit England at about midnight just going into the 16th) and he's got another drawing of the gale's isobars and he said "A woman phoned in, apparently, worried that there is going to be a hurricane; well don't worry, if you're still watching, there isn't." Well there was. And you can Google *Michael Fish storm* and there's a video of him actually saying it. Go to his web site and you'll see it – the most famous moment in television according to England's Channel 5. But it didn't really happen like that!'

'What do you mean?' asked my wife, 'I heard him say it.'

'Yes, I heard him say it and for years I was like millions of other BBC viewers. "Michael Fish said there won't be a hurricane!!!" But let me tell you what actually happened. Michael. Fish was forecasting the weather on the morning shift and a colleague of his had a mother who was going to Florida and she was afraid of a hurricane in Florida.'

'Well that's sensible,' said Frank, 'we get hurricanes in Florida.'

'If I'd said that you'd have told me not to be flippant.' I said to my lady wife.'

'Just get on with it.'

'OK, well instead of him saying a colleague of mine's mother is scared about going to Florida, he just said a woman phoned in worried about a hurricane, blah, blah. And he was right, the tropical storm in the Atlantic didn't develop. He finished his shift and went home. But before he did, he told everybody in England to batten down the hatches against the high winds which were on their way. Michael Fish has been unjustly criticized for seventeen years. It's become his calling card; like I said it's even on his own web site. But he forecast it right. Nobody expected three million damaged homes but that was because of the French.'

'What have the French got to do with it?'

'Their weather forecasters were on strike. So instead of looking at the Bay of Biscay they weren't there, so they didn't tell us what was going on. It was the French.' Anyway, back to the plot. I remember a newscast on the radio as I was driving home that day –

and we were getting 90mph winds, where we lived – and it said "The Worthing School field trip leader is becoming rather concerned."

There's this school teacher out on a school trip, there's 100 plus mile an hour winds, he's got a bus full of kids and the newscaster says he is "becoming rather concerned".

One meteriologist says the Channel will become "very breezy" and the head of field trips "is becoming rather concerned". Don't you just love English understatement?'

'So what happened to you?'

'Well', said Carol, 'we lived at Dronfield Hilltop at the time – the clue is in the place-name – and he gets home and I said

'Where have you left the car?' And he said

'Outside' as though it was the most natural thing to do with a car in 90 mile winds.

So I said 'Don't you think you should move it?

And guess what? He moved it back up the drive away from the house.'

'Well there were tiles coming off the roof and I didn't want them to hit the car.'

'Why didn't you just put it in the garage?' asked Shirl

'I didn't think.'

I could see my wife with one of those *he didn't think* looks on her face. And she followed up with 'Now our driveway was lined with great big English poplars, forty feet high English poplars. Well one of those forty foot high poplars decided to **fall on the blooming car.**

'No!'

'Yessssssss! To stop the car from being hit by a roof tile he positioned it so it could be hit by a tree. It took two days just to saw enough of the tree up to get the car moved – or what was left of it. But, apparently, it wasn't a hurricane; it was only a 111 mile an hour gale – on the Beaufort Scale.'

And for reasons I didn't fully comprehend, everyone looked at me and laughed themselves silly. Frank even patted me on the shoulder. And, after everyone had finished, Roger asked 'Have there been any other breezy days?'

'1990', I said, 'the Burns Night storm.'

'When was that?' He asked

'Well it was Burns Night.' I responded

'January 25th,' Jim chimed in, 'every good Scotsman knows Robbie Burns.

'And before that?'

'Well the 1987 storm was the worst in nearly 300 years. The last really great storm to hit England was in 1703. It's supposed to have lasted from late November to early December. Eight thousand people lost their lives.'

'1703!' exclaimed Shirley, 'America wasn't even a country in 1703.'

'No' I said, 'but the Admiralty still kept proper records. You can always rely on the Navy. 120 mile an hour winds, they reckon. Daniel Defoe wrote his first book about it the next year; it was called *The Storm* (apparently Daniel hadn't developed much imagination when he first started out) and he said "no pen could describe it, no tongue could express it, no thought could conceive it". Given those three statements it was probably a very short book. But the really cool thing is he blamed it on the fact that the English fleet had just lost a major sea battle to France, and it was God's punishment.'

'Seriously? God's punishment for losing a sea battle?'

'Well it was to the French! It was during the *War of Spanish Succession* – it's called Queen Anne's War in American history books. The English fleet got trounced and old Daniel decided the English were being punished for losing. What was left of the fleet after the battle then got destroyed by the storm after they got back to Chatham docks.'

'You didn't park your boat there, by any chance?' Wondered Nancy

'Ow!'

And the conversation got back to Florida and our four hurricanes – one of which was still blowing. For almost fifteen hours Jeanne blew. Fifteen hours of non-stop, persistent wind. It's very tiring listening to all that wind. But that's all it is – wind. No bangs, no crashes, no twisting sounds, no thumps against the house wall. Just wind. And we sat and "visited" and talked and joked about how different things are now but how they'll always be the same. The place still looks all beat up, we all have blue tarps on our roofs, we're all very tired, we still get punctures, we're still all trying to locate good contractors for things we haven't dealt with, yet. The Red Cross has stopped delivering free lunches (at least on our street) and there are still lots of "out-of-towners" cruising around trying to get work or just seeing if there's any aluminum they can collect to sell for scrap. There are still badly damaged homes with signs painted on them telling strangers "I'm home, I'm armed, I'm mad. Don't test me." But we all feel blessed we came out of it so well; we have become a lot closer in a lot of ways.

And this evening our friends and neighbors learned something about English weather and Admiral Beaufort and Burns Night and how the BBC describes impending disasters and how I've never been all that practical. But it really didn't occur to me to put the car in the garage.

And 17 years later I'm living in a new country and I still left my car out. But, at least, this time it was to protect my daughter's car. And all the talk of Michael Fish put me in mind of Lois and Jim. And Dr Seve and Robert. And how happy we are living in our new country. So here I am in Jim's house with the best neighbors in the world listening to everyone tell their stories and I'm wondering –

'Shall I get myself another beer or shall I get Carol to get me another beer?'

The Upside Effect

August 13th Hurricane Charley.
September 5th Hurricane Frances.
September 16th Hurricane Ivan.
September 25th Hurricane Jeanne.
Will things ever be normal? How can there be an upside?
It's still only October and we've had four hurricanes.

The cycle is in motion. Tropical storms build in frequency and intensity for about 20 years and then they subside for about 20 years, making it a 40 year cycle. We went through 20 years of low frequency and low intensity storms. Even when storms did blow they pretty much bypassed our little piece of paradise because we are protected by the Bermuda High and the cold fronts, so we didn't really notice that we are about half way through a "busy cycle".

And 40 years before this cycle no one was even wondering about a "cycle". 80 years ago people thought about other things. 80 years ago Henry Flagler had only recently built his Trans-Florida railroad using the latest material – something called "reinforced concrete", for the bridges. So no one even knew about hurricane cycles let alone try to forecast how long they lasted or what they were linked to – like water temperature or *El Niño*, *La Niña* and even *El Niño Modoki*.

40 years, or so, ago there were fewer than 5 million living in Florida compared with over 18 million living here now. So not many were living in Gulf-front and riverfront communities. There were fewer newspapers and no real television to speak of. Jim and Lois were not on every night reading the news and looking out of the window to see what was happening. And Dr Steve wasn't getting gigabytes of data downloaded from satellites and weather balloons and storm-chaser aircraft and ship-based monitoring stations like today, so a lot of storms went almost unnoticed.

When I was at college – about 40 years ago, by sheer coincidence –

I remember studying meteorology for a couple of hours (well it was raining outside) and learning that tropical storm cycles coincide with the thermo-saline cycle – and **that** was something many scientists were not then able to accept. Scientists, it seems, need to do a lot of studying before they accept something. "Thermo-saline cycle? Not proven." They say.

Well it's flaming well proven as far as I'm concerned.

It seems that the amount of salt in sea water affects water temperature and water temperature, as we so well know, affects air temperature. Hurricanes cannot develop if sea water is less than 70°F. So the less salty the sea, the higher the water temperature; the higher the water temperature, the stronger the hurricanes. Wait until the old ice caps start to really melt and the sea gets lots and lots of freshwater from the melted ice, then we'll see really serious hurricane seasons. I actually remember my lecturer saying that there will be more intense and more frequent storms across the entire world.

Wouldn't you think that something that's very important that *might* be true – like hurricane theory – would at least be wondered about by scientists and politicians and property developers? To say nothing of insurance companies. I wonder if there's a chap sitting in Lloyds of London going "Well didn't **we** underwrite a lot of Gulf Coast insurance policies? Could we have added a few restrictions like we'll insure homes and offices and stores if . . . (fill in the blank) . . . so not only do we not lose lots of money in insurance claims but also the damage from hurricanes will be less." That would have made sense, wouldn't it?

Why do some things have to "proven" before they get serious consideration?

To my simple mind, before there were lots of motor cars on the road and Mrs Jameson had just been run over (she was the very first person in history to be run over by a motor car – if you didn't already know that it'll probably come up in 'Millionaire' or something) it must have occurred to someone to say that more cars will mean more accidents. More accidents will mean more anguish and less productive work (if only by the person who gets run over)

The Upside Effect

so let's have rules for cars and pedestrians.

And I'll bet there was a scientist somewhere going "Not proven; more cars don't necessarily mean more accidents. We don't need to plan for that eventuality until there is a graph plotting increase in cars, increase in pedestrians and an increase in accidents." I'll bet there was. I'll bet some scientist took off his sensible head and wore his has-to-be- proven-by-science head and some people will have said "Well he is a scientist, so he must know what he's talking about." Or did people just say "Yeah, that makes sense, let's have road rules before too many people get run over."

Now I know that road rules don't stop everyone from getting hit by cars but it was right to have rules just in case. And I think we should have rules "just in case" there are lots of hurricanes every 40 years (whether the ice caps melt ot not). To me "highest and best use" isn't always a bigger home or an office building instead of a parking lot, or a high rise condo development instead of a strip mall. "Highest and best use" is sometimes "trees".

Trees? Yes, let me explain (if you are a budding scientist and you don't want to keep up you can skip this bit – but it's really important). Take mangroves, for example. There were far more mangroves 40 years ago than there are today.

"What have mangroves got to do with it?" I hear you cry.

Well, mangroves grow in shallow saltwater. Mangroves form a kind of see-through hurricane barrier and so they protect against storm surge like man-made barriers (such as houses and office buildings) never can. High water blown by strong wind just keeps going and going and going. Then the streets flood and people's houses flood and stores and offices flood.

And insurance companies get the next boat out of Dodge.

Well if you have millions of mangrove roots and knees and branches in the way, the surge might be much less, so you get less flooding. They can also slow the wind at ground level by up to 20 miles an hour. Now when our local TV meteorologists talk about wind-shear destroying hurricanes they are talking about crosswinds 20,000 plus feet up in the air. But anything at ground level that takes the bottom off the wind, instead of the top, would be good wouldn't it?

Well wouldn't it?

So "mangrove-shear" should reduce wind speed. Slow the wind and lessen the storm surge and you should have less property damage. So less property damage means less cost and less disruption to everyone's lives and so we can all get back to work sooner and make the money we're not making because we can't go to work because of all the damage. (I think there's an economics doctorate degree waiting for the person who can prove the science of that). So where it's sensible to, plant new mangroves and leave other mangroves in place in front of the buildings and "bingo" we're all safer and happier and making money. As long as there are enough mangroves, of course.

And the insurance companies might not be pulling out of Florida and Florida tax payers might not be picking up the tab through Citizens' Insurance. And if we didn't have to fund the State insurance cover perhaps we could have lower taxes (even if they're called "fees" or "supplements"). But, of course, there are so many people currently living in water front areas we can't just wade in a plant mangrove forests; it will take thinking and planning to keep everyone happy. But if we can put a man on the moon and consider putting one on Mars, there's got to be a way of reducing the effect of wind and flood without spoiling the lives of those who live in water front communities. Let's go back to motor cars for a moment.

The downside of road safety is slower vehicular traffic, more stop lights, more yield signs and more actual areas where vehicles are not allowed – like sidewalks. If there were no sidewalks there'd be more room for vehicles. But sidewalks and stop lights and yield signs are actually good for everybody. Nobody considers rules of the road as excessive government interference; nobody considers sidewalks to be "not the highest and best use" of potential road space (do they?). Road safety is good for everybody. And the reason everyone accepts it is probably just because it's always been like that.

Hurricane safety and flood safety is also good for everybody, It's just that nobody thought about it this way before because nobody realized the thermo-saline cycle had much to do with "me and my home" on a very windy and very wet day.

And another thing.

I always hate that – and another thing – it's what my ever-loving says after I think the argument is over. We have an argument (like about not evacuating before a hurricane) and I think it's all over and I start to relax and she says "And another thing . . ." and I have to gear up, again, for more, undoubtedly useful information about why I am not the perfect man I tend to assume I am.

So – here's another thing:-

Roads, everywhere, lose their street lights and utility poles to hurricanes. Thousands and thousands of street lights lie across the road. They are all over the place, street light after street light, utility pole after utility pole all lie in the road, slowing traffic (and not in a good way). While the poles were down there's no electricity in homes and offices and stores.

Now then, if my theory is correct "trees" could have been the answer. Look at the trees that come down in hurricanes – which ones? The tall ones, the ones all on their own, the isolated ones. Trees don't come down in a haphazard, random sort of way; there's a pattern to it. Go and stand in an area of fallen trees. What do you see? Palmettos and small trees are OK, big old hollow trees are OK, stands of tall trees very close together are, generally, OK but look at the trees on their own; look at the tall pines that aren't very close together – broken off 12 to 20 feet up the trunk. Why?

Let me explain (I'm also aiming for a doctorate in wind dynamics, not just in economics). What caused those trees to break half way up? What caused the street lights to come off at the base? Wind, that's what. (Yes, I know; it's a hurricane).

Let's start with the trees. Trees are flexible; they bend, and sway in the wind, sucked this way and that. (For budding wind physicists, winds don't blow trees down, they suck them down – honestly). Strong wind moves more slowly at ground level (coefficient of friction) than higher up. At ground level the tree is better supported and the wind is less powerful.

At 12 to 20 feet the wind suffers no ground friction, so it's actually faster and the tree is less well supported – so it suffers from vacuum-fatigue (my science) and it breaks. And so do the street lights and utility poles. The street lights come off at the base because they're designed to snap off at base level.

So how do we help the humble utility pole and the humble street light? (Thanks for asking) Trees, that's how.

Plant trees round each pole and street light – clumps of palmetto or bougainvillea, or hibiscus, or whatever, on the perimeter of the clump (another scientific term), and 10 to 20 foot-high trees closest to the poles. 4 trees to a pole and each tree has to be at least 4 feet from the pole. These taller trees should have branches beginning at least 8 feet from the ground. And what you get is an "eddy zone" round each pole. A kind of hurricane reduction zone (or HRZ if you're reading this and still in CERN).

So – if we can slow ground level winds with mangroves at the coast (and out into shallow water and keep the winds slowed with palmettos and such by putting "eddy zones" round each utility pole, street light, cell phone tower and other static vertical object (SVO), we could save up to, let's guess at, half of all street lights and utility poles. And that saves money, work effort and recovery time.

We all win. (Upside). So, just a thought; just a little scientific application to help us through the next 40 years. And on top of that we get more attractive streets. Everybody likes to see flowers and trees. Because everybody likes beauty. (Upside)

So how do we pay for all of these beautification projects? How do we get every street light and utility pole "adopted"? Without raising taxes? Dead easy (maybe).

Mayor Koch (I think) sold pot holes in the streets of New York City. Pay to fill a pot hole and you get a photograph of it with your name on it and a Valentine card goes to your loved one (or a Christmas or Hanukkah or Ramadan card. Or birthday or father's day or boss's day or anything-else-we-celebrate card). That would pay for it. (Upside).

Or here's another way – civics lessons in schools could include a credit on *"the social contribution and municipal cost-saving effect of nature-based hurricane reduction zones"* (the title, alone, is worth a credit). But to get the credit you and your fellow students would actually have to create at least one HRZ i.e. plant some trees and shrubs round lights and utility poles. (More community Upside)

When I was at high school I did a whole course in agricultural science and we planted things all the time just to make the school look nice when visitors came. (When we weren't learning about cow stomachs and grass). It was fun, we got fit – you get fit just by digging holes for trees, we learned a lot about plants and how to look after them (and I got to drive a tractor) and school pride went through the stratosphere – especially for kids who didn't play sports. And then we started growing plants to put in front of buildings that weren't even in school. Just because we wanted to; planting and digging holes was fun. And it never occurred to anyone that there might be some kind of wind mitigation effect as a bonus (not too many hurricanes where I grew up – there's another old joke there, but I know you're ahead of me).

Or, just to be controversial, we could move to a system of *social contribution* instead of *pointless punishment*. Instead of doing ordinary community service which just gets litter picked up or something, let's have miscreants creating HRZ's around SVO's. County jails and State penitentiaries are full of people who occasionally clean roads or clean out swales. So what else could they do?

They could grow shrubs and trees, that's what (Upside). And just to incentivize it, how about time off for every plant that makes it to the "zone". (It takes time to grow a tree until it is big enough for the zone, so it's not too easy an option. Time off for good behavior, time off for growing a tree). Everyone (almost) likes to feel a sense of achievement, so here's a way to offer folk an opportunity to feel good about themselves and to contribute, in a simple but effective way, to the society to which they owe a debt.

Or what about this? We're all familiar with "Adopt-a-road". So how about: Adopt-a-hurricane-reduction-zone? Give your free time if you are a family, a street, a block or a club. And we all get to live in a more attractive place that is going to withstand strong winds more effectively, suffer less flooding from storm surge, sustain less damage and less disruption. We can all get on with our normal lives more quickly, we all would pay less in insurance premiums (maybe) and we all save tax dollars. (Upside). Instead of money going to the State to pay for insurance cover that commercial companies won't write policies on, instead of our utility bills going up to pay for the replacement utility poles, all that money could either be saved or put straight back into the local economy – local to wherever you live.

Is that an Upside or what?

Everyone comes together to help everyone else after storms take away our "normal" lives. Many, many people help others every day of every year by working with charities and civic associations and clubs. We are, naturally, a helpful country, a nation of "neighbors". It's one of the reasons I so wanted to immigrate to America, it's a nation of neighbors and I love that.

Neighbors helping neighbors; that has huge motivational power. The few weeks of hurricanes and danger and pain brought out the very best in thousands upon thousands of people. Every disaster does that; people help people. So let's keep it going. Let's look to the future. Let's all be hurricane heroes and do something to reduce the impact of the next natural disaster. Let's plant trees or increase mangrove spread in shallow water, let's save a utility pole or save a street light, let's make our communities more beautiful, more disaster-resistant, more safe. Let's get them ready for the next strong wind, the next flood, the next whatever. As individuals, families, clubs and neighborhoods we can make a huge difference.

And on a much larger scale local governments, local businesses and planning authorities could contribute so much to reinvigorating, beautifying and strengthening the infrastructure of whole communities – just look at some of the urban plans available on the Internet which shows so clearly how whole towns and cities want to plan for future growth. And in five years time, say in 2009, wouldn't it be great to look at our communities and see the new beauty and the new strength?

The Upside Effect

What a wonderful challenge for us all. What a great Upside.

And on a more personal level, we all have "honey-do" lists; fix this, clean out that, repaint the other. Some people enjoy doing chores and some don't. I'm in the group who don't. To me a chore is a chore; I'm not practical and I'm not neat and tidy but I realized that by nailing down that piece of loose fascia board and by clearing the holes in the drain line on the pool deck I wasn't just checking off another thing on my list. What I was doing was making my home stronger against high wind and less likely to flood if heavy rains come my way. Suddenly that list of chores turned into me protecting my family. And that made me feel good.

Millions of us live in homes built to an older "code". We might live in older, weaker homes but they're still our *homes*. They are where we live, where we bring up our children, where we make memories, where we spend winters, where we build our retirement money through increased property values. We can take that "honey-do" list a step further; don't just fix something that needs fixing, find a way to make it better than it was before. By improving our own homes we can make them stronger and safer – for ourselves and our families.

Instead of just "preparing in case there's another one" let's look ahead and actually <u>improve</u> our homes so they're better places in which to live, bring up our children, enjoy our retirement or vacations and make memories.

A lot of insurance-paid repair work resulted in many homes being "brought up to code". That makes them better homes, more comfortable and more valuable. And many older commercial buildings that got destroyed got rebuilt to new code. What a great opportunity to make them more attractive, as well.

I don't want to suffer another hurricane and I don't want anyone to go through hurricanes, floods, wild fires or any other disaster. But if there are going to be such things we can expect that one result could be a better community and better homes. And I know that previous disasters in other parts of the country had one very specific result – property values increased. And that's definitely an Upside.

So, let's use our brains and our hearts and our community spirit and build some real and long-lasting Upside! Let's work with each other to agree low-cost ways of making our communities safer and more attractive. And let's see if the end result is lots of good looking communities, less storm damage, lower insurance premiums, higher property values and happier homes.

Before we can mobilize whole communities to make our homes safer and stronger let's start with ourselves – each and every one of us. Let's look at everything that could be done to maximize the chances of minimal damage. And let's look at how we, as individuals and families can inspire each other and empower ourselves by thinking about all the little things we can actually do. Let's think about some bigger things as well. Let's list out every single thing that will be good for us, our family members, our pets, our homes, our boats – and then let's do them!

I've put together lists of over 350 different actions. They cover everything I can think of to protect people, pets and property. And as I was doing it I found myself saying 'I could have done this', or 'So-and-so really needed to do that' and I also thought 'I did *that*' and 'I did *that* as well'. 'I never even thought of doing *that*!'

And the more I worked on putting these lists together, the better I felt. And I realized that just having these lists made me feel good. And I added to the practical lists by including emotional and spiritual things – And that made me feel even better.

When I reviewed all the things that need to be done or, at least, thought about I said to myself 'Tony, this is amazing, this is everything you need. And just think how much money they're all worth I felt so strong, so ready, so powerful. And I knew that preparedness was more than what you do a few days before a storm or a couple of weeks into "the season". Preparedness is doing those jobs around the house knowing they actually mean more than being just "a repair job". Calling an insurance agent to discuss coverage isn't just about wondering if you can afford the premium or if it's worth it. Making that call is about knowing whatever way you decide it's the right way for you and your family. Teaching your young children how to make a 911 call or arranging with an out of state relative who will be your central contact in case of emergency can save a life or a broken heart at any time of the year.

Preparedness is about what's inside you as well as what you do; it's how you feel; it's being able to tell your family "We're *UP* for anything *the Future* can throw at us. We're ready!" And that's a great way to be!

Be prepared! – Think ahead, plan ahead

We're riding along on the crest of a wave
And the sun is in the sky!
We've all our eyes on
The distant horizon
Look out for passers-by!

I loved being a Boy Scout it taught me so much about learning to become so much better than I was. And so much is summed up in *The Motto* "Be Prepared" and in *The Promise*, which begins "On my honor I promise to do my best to do my duty . . ."

"To do my best" – what a great approach to everything.

And that's what this section is about – doing our best by being prepared. Prepare properly and you're ahead of the game as I and so many thousands of others learned in that strange period called *after the disaster*.

I'm not a hurricane expert; I'm a hurricane veteran. A veteran of the worst storm to hit my State since Hurricane Andrew 12 years before. Charley killed 34 people and caused $13billion in damage. And it was the worst to hit my County since Hurricane Donna 44 years earlier. So I don't know everything but I do know enough to know it pays to be prepared better than I was and better than many of my neighbors and friends were.

I also know that the "hurricane cycle" is a fickle thing. How many people have said to you "We're going into an El Niño year, so we'll be OK." Well, guess what – **Hurricane Andrew** and **Hurricane Alicia** both destroyed a huge whole heck of a lot in *El Niño years!* Hurricanes are fickle things!

I also know that as well as hurricanes everyone one of us can be threatened by other natural disasters. For example, in 2007, **every state in the Union suffered from flooding**. Along with hurricanes (or just heavy rain or snow melt come floods.

In the past hundred years or so, in the US, about 1000 people

every year have drowned in floods. And then there are wildfires and tornadoes and earthquakes.

Each type of natural disaster brings its own special problems but – and I'm sure of this – the better the forward plan the better for all concerned. Regardless of the disaster we all have someone or something we want to protect whether it's family, pets, friends, neighbors, homes, schools, places of business. Being prepared is a good thing!

If you and family described in a few sentences how you would like to feel before, during and after a natural disaster – what would you all say?

"Safe from harm"

"Confident we have the provisions we'll need"

"Agreed on the conditions that will make us evacuate"

"Clear about when, where and how we'll evacuate"

"Comfortable our children understand as much as they can about what to do, etc."

"Secure in the belief that our children will stay strong through it all"

"Satisfied about our post-disaster follow-up actions."

I think that's what *Begin with the end in mind* actually means. And you really do have to "stay sharp". Each day is an opportunity to learn how to be better than you might have been or even better than you were. As you go through disaster preparation and the aftermath keep learning – keep sharpening that saw! And imagine if you could confront the likelihood of a natural disaster coming your way with words like *Safe, Confident, Agreed, Clear, Secure, Satisfied* and *Comfortable*. How fantastic would that be?

They're words you don't see very often in the disaster preparation guides. All the guides I've read cover a lot of points and are fairly detailed when it comes to <u>what</u> to do and even <u>how</u> to do it. They are full of really useful information.

But I think some critically important things are missing.

So I wanted to try to put all the ideas together and to add

something extra – as a hurricane veteran who wishes he'd done a better job the first time and hoping you'll benefit for next time! Whatever the "disaster" is that you're preparing for. This whole section is designed to help you feel inspired and to feel empowered.

I've also added things to the list that don't need to wait until "hurricane season" "fire season" or even until the newscaster says "It's on its way folks".

Some things to do are things we should do just because we're responsible home owners and good family members. Now if you're anything like me and not very good with screwdrivers it's not the end of the world; it's not even the end of you having a quiet mind.

Many of the things I believe you should do are really simple – and really effective. Everybody puts things off and not being good with tools is a great excuse for putting things off. But that's all it is – an excuse. Think of it in terms of "you against the disaster". I know that after the first hurricane hit I wished I could have turned the clock back just one day, even, so I could have done some very simple things that didn't occur to me. Things like save my mailbox or my water softener lid or my mains water pipe. And what would it have taken? Unscrewing two screws would have saved my mailbox and no tools at all to save my water softener lid and water pipe. But because I didn't think well enough it cost me and my family several days longer without water coming into the house than it needed to and it cost about $60 to repair the pipe and buy a new mailbox. $60 down the drain. $60 I could have saved. I tell you, if someone had said "Go and get your mailbox, bring in the softener lid and don't forget the hosepipe" I'd have had an extra $60 today. And that's just a quick example of how this section will save you money. Simple things like that, simple, easy and obvious things so many people I know "didn't think about" And those simple things, alone, will add up to hundreds of dollars.

Some of the ideas will be worth thousands of dollars – and you'll also save time, effort and heartache. This is a good section!

I'm going to focus on hurricanes because they deliver two of the main types of damage – wind and flood. As I said, I know wildfires and earthquakes are very different but in terms of "before the disaster", "evacuating to a safe place" and "after the disaster" I believe there are lots of similarities.

I've never met anyone who is living where a Federal Disaster has been declared telling me that a disastrous "this" is better or worse than a disastrous "that"!

Regardless of what disaster you and your family are preparing for you still want to feel safe, confident, clear, comfortable, secure and whatever other words or terms you and your family relate to.

And you still need to cope with the aftermath of living through your particular disaster. So, yes, they're different but there's still lots of similarities.

And as the warden in *Cool Hand Luke* said – you've got to get your mind right.

So let's do that, let's get our minds right, so we're "up" for the *before part*, the *during part* and the *after part* of the disaster.

We'll cover **wind and flood specifics separately**, that way you should get as much out of this as easily and quickly as possible. I've laid out the action steps into clear sections, **so you can go straight to the part you want**.

At the end of the section, in the Appendix, you'll see the names of useful organizations (like FEMA, Red Cross, Salvation Army) and how to contact them. There is so much detail available to deal with very specific issues that I suggest you start with these sources and go from there. Having said that, the vast majority of people and families need the more general and more obvious.

The more I thought, looked and researched, the more I realized that there didn't seem to be **a single source of ideas, strategies actions and good old-fashioned tips**. That's why I put this section together – **to make it easier and quicker to do what needs to be done**. And most of the "official" sources seem to ignore the background, underlying issues and they focus on the "what" and "how" tasks. I am absolutely convinced that to be really ready your mind and spirit have to be ready – if you fully intend to be "Up" for the disaster you are preparing for.

Things to do a long time before you are threatened

Family things
- Have a **family meeting** to discuss what you will all do if a disaster threatens. Ask children, especially young ones, what their thoughts are and what, if anything, they are frightened or worried about. Talking helps "the unknown" to be less frightening
- **Give everyone a copy of YOUR FAMILY'S Disaster Preparation list.** Change its name to make it personal so the whole family feels involved in looking after each other, their home and their pets.

You might already have done some of the things on the list (how safe the property is re building code, knowing your insurance is up to date, etc.) In this way you can be satisfied your children will feel safer, so they can focus on the practical things they can do to help and to stay focused. Just as long as you tell them about how strong their home is and that you've checked the insurance is up to date, just in case.

- **Pre-pay monthly bills** in case you can't pay them when they are due. (It might save you a "late charge")
- When you **discuss evacuation plans**, you can ask the children for suggestions about where you could go, who you might use as an out-of-area contact (family members or friends in another state) etc.
- One child might like to be the one who asks that person if they will be **the contact** and then can make sure all family members have the phone number. It's simple things like this which helps children to know they are useful members of the "team"
- One child could be in charge of getting things ready for the **family pet**

Things to do a long time before you are threatened

- Each child can be responsible for putting their own **"emergency pack"** together in case of evacuation

- Start a **"Family File"**. Each person gets their own section. Each page of the file lists things to do, things to have, etc. And each person can add thoughts and ideas as they occur to them, so good ideas or things to do get on the list and so they get done. Words like "meant to" or "forgot to" have no place in your day when you're preparing to ward off a disaster. And, of course, the file can be kept and used year after year

- **If**, when the time comes, **you are in a building which begins to fail** you might be forced to leave it. Prepare an emergency evacuation plan – have at least 2 ways of leaving the building

- More importantly discuss such a plan with your county **Emergency Management**. They will have specific thoughts that could save your life

- **Have a "Family Treasure Chest of Strength"**

  Suggest that you have a family **"prayer for the day"** or a **"thought for the day"** or a **"word for the day"** so that, before an impending disaster, and after it has passed, the family stays "on course".

  The children can contribute to prayers, thoughts and words. Each child can write down what they want to be used on a given day. Each day one of their note pages can be taken from the "family treasure chest of strength" to be read and used. Words such as "strength", "focus", "cheerfulness" are good words to help everyone, especially children, to know that they will get through the disaster's aftermath.

  Let's say one of the words of the day is "cheerfulness" – useful to remember when fatigue kicks in – sing a song, smile at each other at least three times, say "Thank you" for something good. These are simple ways to help each family member stay cheerful and stand tall no matter how badly the home might have been damaged. You can't undo the damage, so you've got to live through the aftermath – I'm just suggesting these ideas might help.

And they are easy things to remind each other about, so that everyone does stay on track. If a family member begins to feel depressed or angry or frustrated, the conversation can include "our prayer", "our thought" or "our word" for the day. It's just a good place to start the conversation and should help that person refocus.

And it can have the added benefit of enabling that person to think of a new prayer, thought or word to add to the family's treasure chest. Younger children might even want to draw a picture to display their thoughts or feelings – now your family will have a "picture of the day" as well.

- Agree what you'll all use as the **safe room**, so children will be OK when it comes to squeezing into the closet

- Make sure your children know how to use phones and cell phones, do texting, etc. AND that they **can dial 911**. And they know what to say

   You can **role-play those calls**. Even if there's no natural disaster this year, how many news items have you seen where a young child saved the family because they handled the 911 call correctly?

- Take a **basic first aid class**, learn how to do CPR. Again, even if you don't need such skills because of a hurricane or flood, you might become someone's hero next week, next month, next year!

   I honestly believe that the aftermath can have a "heavy" effect on people's emotions. If it didn't there would be many more smiling faces, less anger and a lot fewer arguments – and even fewer fights in the days following the disaster.

- Form a **support group** of friends and neighbors (or co-workers, fellow club members, etc.) so you and your whole community get fully prepared. Even if you all just add something to your community spirit, it's a great feeling to know you are all "there" for each other

- If someone has **special needs** this is the time to agree who can help if you become unavailable, hurt or ill
- **Get fit!**

If you aren't fit you will really ache and get really tired if a disaster hits. If gyms and fitness videos are your thing – Great! If not (like me) get a 15 minute routine going to tone a few muscles. But, obviously, see a physician before you begin anything new when it comes to exercise

Big, practical things

Decide how well your home might stand up to the possible disaster event. You know your area and what disaster you most want to prepare for – high winds, flooding, wildfire, earthquake. As far as practical things to do I'm going to focus on wind and water.

Will your home meet current **wind mitigation standards**?

Call your County Building Codes Department or your home owner insurance agent or a licensed building inspector. Get a **wind mitigation inspection**. Then correct as much as you can

Get help from a local (licensed) building contractor, building supplies store or your county Emergency Management Office (EMO).

Is your property in a **Special Flood Hazard Area**? Your home owner insurance agent can help you. Or call your county Emergency Management Office and ask them.

Making your home stronger and safer

There are **a lot of things** you can do, yourself, to help make your home stronger and safer. And they might get you a lower insurance premium!

By planning and thinking ahead you might just **save yourself a lot of heartache and post-disaster expense** – especially if your insurance cover is less than it might be.

Hire **a licensed contractor** to do the work, as appropriate.

But here's a list you should find useful.

Review the fix-ups and repairs we covered earlier – and do them.

Get lengths of 2x4's and use them to **brace your roof and trusses** and gable ends (take advice as I mentioned to decide if you should use 2x4's or 1x6's or get a contractor to do it).

Add **tie-downs** (straps or clips) to help keep the roof intact. If you believe you already have tie-downs, check (or have them checked) that they are there and properly installed.

If you have **sky lights** on the roof, can they be made more secure in time of high wind? Check to ensure they are water tight and reseal them.

If you've got **roof turbines or window A/C units** find out how to remove them and how to protect the space where they were.

Garage doors are big and take a lot of buffeting by high winds. If the garage door fails, your home fails! A reputable garage door company can install bracing to help the door withstand high winds (and they're cheaper than buying a new door). The very least you should do is decide how you will brace the door in some other way. A lot of folk I know backed their cars up behind the door. Make sure you cushion the car with blankets, etc. so if the door bends in and out it won't scratch the car too much. But that's not as effective as retro-fitted storm bracing by a licensed supplier.

Protect your windows!

You can do everything from replacing the windows with impact rated glass, fitting shutters or panels.

Or buy plywood – at least 5/8 of an inch thick. Measure the windows (obviously) get the store to cut the wood then drill holes.

And buy appropriate screws (and washers). If the wood is held by something just the size of a screw head it can be torn off, more easily, in a high wind. Big old washers add a lot of extra strength

BUT remember – a Cat 5 hurricane (or even a Cat 4 with higher wind gusts) where winds exceed 155mph can blow debris fast enough to puncture plywood. Travelling at 35mph a "hurricane cannonball" can go straight through plywood, straight through the

Things to do a long time before you are threatened

window and straight through whoever it hits!

I'm told that sticking duct tape onto windows has no effect; the window will still smash if struck by flying debris, the glass will still shatter.

I'm also told that it takes a looooong time to get it off the windows afterwards and it can damage any window film (to keep out UV rays, etc.) already on the glass. (But check with a good home improvement store or your county EMO advisor.)

Fit the shutters, panels or plywood **as a practice run**, especially if you own a newer home and have never fitted the panels that came with the house. I know a few people whose panels were the wrong size – find out now!

Double doors are much weaker than single doors. The bolts locking the door you don't use (everyone just uses one of the doors) might be rusted or weak. Test them and replace them. If the store suggests the new bolt still won't be strong enough fit hurricane-resistant protection. At very least fit a "burglar bar" or other strengthening device.

Some thoughts about insurance

If you have insurance cover, check it so you know exactly what is covered (most people don't read the little pamphlets which we get sent by the company).

If you don't have insurance cover, check it out. It doesn't cost anything to get a quote. The premium will depend on a lot of factors – one of them is how much deductible you will carry. My thought is that if you have no insurance and you get "hit", you're responsible for all the costs of repair. If you have insurance and a high deductible (to keep the premium down) you're responsible for less of the cost of repair – check it out and decide.

If you rent where you live now you can get "renters' insurance" for your personal possessions; it's a lot cheaper than regular home owner insurance. If you have a mortgage can you get payment cover if you can't work because your place of employment got destroyed?

Flood insurance is very cheap compared with home owner cover. It starts at about $120 a year. I'm told that any form of rising water is "a flood" (like sewer back-up or rain water being blown under your front door – and that might not be covered by your regular home owner insurance. Speak to your agent because some home owner policies do cover sewer back-up. And some do not.

Now put that into perspective. Let's say you don't take out flood insurance; it costs, say $300 for the year. And let's say you get 1inch of flood water – 1 inch of flooding, according to FEMA, will cost just under $8000 to repair – carpets, base boards, drywall. What about 12 inches of flood water? You just spent $20,000 in round numbers to repair. You can save a lot of money with insurance. And flood insurance starts at $120! At very least, check it out.

If you have a mortgage there are a couple of things to think about – do you have payment cover? If you lose your income do you carry insurance so your mortgage is still paid? Some credit cards offer this; you might be paying for it without knowing. If you don't have that kind of cover, see what it costs, it might be worth it to you.

The other thing is that your mortgage company will be named on any insurance pay out. The mortgage company will have to co-endorse your insurance checks before they can be deposited in your bank account. Some lenders actually control how that payout money is used. As an example they might require that some goes towards your mortgage. Check it out, so you know. It might be worth arranging a line of credit on your home to cover immediate payments for repairs, etc. If your lender either does require insurance payouts to be allocated to your mortgage or if the office which signs off on the check is in another state and you have to mail it to them.

If you own a business you might want to consider loss of profits insurance – especially if the bills will keep coming in after a disaster.

If you do suffer from a natural disaster one of the big decisions you have to make is – will you work direct with your insurer or will you have a public loss adjuster represent you. Find out what a public loss adjuster will do for you, what the advantages and benefits are. Many people have never thought about hiring an adjuster. Think about it, now; look in your telephone book and talk to one (or more) so you can make a decision based on prior knowledge rather than making a "quick" decision soon after a disaster hits.

- Check with your insurance agent **what pre-disaster records** they will need to compare with post-disaster damage Do they want photographs, what detail will they expect to see in those photographs? Will they want serial numbers of items you've had to throw out? That kind of thing don't guess – ask

- Then take **lots of photographs** and make your lists of model and serial numbers to show the loss adjuster what it was like before the disaster.

Two more thoughts

- If you **might use a public shelter** get phone numbers, addresses, know how to get there, plan the route you'll take, know their rules so when you get there you can get in (see evacuation notes, below)

- If you are someone with **special needs** or are responsible for **someone who is in hospital, an assisted living facility, etc.** work with the management so everything is clear and organized (see special needs notes, below).

Ready, get set, save

Save money by really getting this part right!
- **Collect discount coupons.** Go to stores' web sites for additional savings, some offer free samples of new items so when you do stock up on things they'll be cheaper
- If you are going to buy hurricane shutters, or other big ticket item **watch** the advertisements **for discounted pricing**
- If you buy prescription medicine check to see if any supermarkets will offer a **discount card** to persuade you to change to their pharmacy
- **Save soda bottles** for your after-the-storm water supply. These bottles are less likely to split when frozen, the ice will keep your freezer colder after the power goes out and you can drink the tap water you filled them with (why buy bottled water if you don't need to?)
- **Repair anything on the outside** of your home that you've been meaning to! (Things like gate and door latches, loose fascia boards, missing soffits; anything that might weaken your home in a storm) **Not** having to replace a whole gate or kill vermin that climb in through the holes where the soffits used to be costs less than if you do have to do those things
- **Trim the trees** so the big old branches won't hit your home if they blow around or break off. And get rid of any coconuts or other big fruit that become "hurricane cannonballs". If this were the only thing to damage your home, by getting rid of it now you'll save money later

    The traditional "hurricane haircut" needs some thought – lopping off too much can harm a tree (then you have to spend money on a replacement). Your County should have some info to help you trim properly
- Tie down the **outdoor shed**. It's probably not covered by

insurance, so save it from as much damage as possible. Ropes and wooden stakes might be all you need to stop it from taking off

- Tie down the **A/C condenser**, so it doesn't shift in high winds. You can buy specific tie-straps for A/C units. If it shifts and breaks you lose your A/C. And you have to pay to have it repaired. Tie-downs are a lot less money

- Find out where the **main water shut-off** is – and that it actually shuts off (instead of being rusted solid). If you evacuate you want to make sure a burst pipe inside your home won't cause a flood

- Do the same for all your utility supply lines. Make sure your family members know, as well, in case you're not there when needed

- **Install hook-and-eye bolts** (or similar) to your roof space access points – usually in garage and a bedroom closet. High wind blowing through the roof space can suck the cover up and cause a lot of mess with windblown debris (like fiber glass insulation) which then has to be cleaned up and might cost a lot more money than a few hook-and-eye bolts

- **Buy** (or borrow) **screwdrivers**, **drills**, etc. to do the fix-up jobs

- **Clean the chimney** if you have a real coal or wood-burning fireplace (soot makes a real mess when it falls)

- Get a **car emergency kit** in case you have to evacuate (tire repair aerosols, booster cables, spare fan belts, bulbs, that kind of thing)

Preparing the pool

Almost everyone has an opinion about how to prepare your pool for a storm. Should you drain your pool? Should you cut the pool cage screens? Well here's my list; again based on my own experience and on what people who know more about pools than I do have told me.

Make sure the **deck drain** is functioning as well as possible. If any of the little drain slots are blocked, clear them. Use a screwdriver (it's that word again!) to poke dirt, old paint, whatever, to make holes for water to drain through. Heavy rain needs to drain away from your home, not into it. If it gets under your door and into your home it's a "flood" and might need specific flood insurance. So help the water drain away.

If your deck doesn't have a drain line make sure that overgrown weeds, grass and so on at the edge of the deck won't act as a kind of dam. If you think you should – cut a trench to help the water drain away.

If you've never experienced huge amounts of rain, get a hosepipe and imitate a storm to see if you get bad puddling or if your drain, say, is blocked somewhere outside your deck area that causes it to back up and flood your lanai. I know of a couple who were out in a Category 1 hurricane trying to stop the rain from coming into their house. All I'm saying is it would have been better to check on the drain the day before!

Don't drain your pool. The overflow should be handled by the drain. If you empty too much water from your pool the pressure of the earth (which will get even more with all the rain) could damage the pool shell – and that will be very expensive to fix.

I wouldn't cut the pool cage screens, either. If the wind isn't too strong, you'll have to buy new screen, an installation device and refit it (or pay someone else to). If the wind is strong enough, it will blow debris into the screen and that will cut the screens for you.

Before the storm arrives, **'shock' the pool**; super-chlorinate it. The rain will encourage algae to grow (and that's another $30+ to kill it, in my experience). You can ask your pool store what you might add as well as "shock" – share the cost with neighbors. If you have a vinyl or fiberglass pool make sure you add the appropriate chemicals.

Store items which could get blown around and become "hurricane cannonballs". If you can't store them inside put them in the pool.

And that's put, don't drop – you might scratch the pool surface. Do not put anything in a vinyl or fiberglass pool because they almost certainly will damage the surface. Do not put metal or glass objects in the pool. They'll scratch the surface and if the glass breaks you'll have a tough time getting every bit of glass out.

Immediately before the storm, turn off the power to the pool, so that if the motor gets damaged there won't be any power going to loose or damaged cables.

Your emergency supplies kit

The first thing to do is to check your *Emergency Supplies Kit* list. Check off what you already have.

Discuss the list with your family in case they have ideas about what else to get. If a child wants something that might help them to feel good about things, try and get it for them.

Discuss with friends and neighbors what you can share. Take plastic sheeting, for example; one roll will be more than you need, probably, to seal damaged soffits, so share the cost and share the product with neighbors. Buy one staple gun between you. Think about the "little" ways you can save money.

Or barrier spray to keep bugs out – one bottle of Talstar® Professional, or similar, will protect, perhaps, 10 homes for 3 months. That makes it cheaper and more effective than a single spray bottle of something you'd see in a supermarket.

Personal and family things

You decide in which order you get the things you need. Some things you'll already have, some you can get as you plan ahead and some will wait until you really need them – like perishable items, extra gas or, say, extra cash.

Some things are more "nice to have" than "got to have" – you choose.

General things

- **Important Documents** (keep them safe and in one place)
- **Large, waterproof, sealable container** for the documents – a cooler is ideal; you can seal it with duct tape and it will float in case of flood

Your emergency supplies kit

- **Extra keys** – house, car, etc. in case you need to leave them with anyone. (Much cheaper than someone having to call out a locksmith)
- Extra **cash** (small bills and coins for public telephones) or **travelers checks** credit and charge card machines might not work for days afterwards. You can also order checks from your credit card company to use instead of a credit card (check to see how they will charge you for using them)
- **Fire extinguisher** – it's good to have one in the kitchen, anyway (If you've already got one check it out to make sure it will still work)
- **Paper and pencil** (or freebie pens)
- **Books, games, playing cards**, etc. for relaxation and to keep kids occupied
- **Whistle or air horn** in case you are injured and not visible (cars and passengers do get washed away in floods) Remember the international distress signal is 3 long blasts – pause – 3 long blasts – pause – 3 etc.

Car and travel prep

- **Gas cans** (and gas) for the car and generator. Remember storing gasoline is dangerous and it goes bad if stored for too long. And also remember that **many gas stations have their own generators**, so getting gas shouldn't be a huge problem (with cash, not cards)
- **Fill your car** before the storm approaches, so you have a full tank
- **Tire repair** aerosols (for all those punctured tires because of all the debris) some brands are cheaper than others. Remember these only work for minor tire damage
- "Star" style **Wheel brace** to get lug nuts off in case of bad puncture. And this is a good time to make sure the jack and tire

irons are there – and you know how to use them; a dark night in the rain during mandatory evacuation is not the best way to learn (believe me!)

- **Car repair/maintenance kit** like spare oil, fan belt, battery charger, water for radiator
- **Jumper cables**
- **Local, State and regional maps**
- **Get your car serviced** and safety-checked ahead of having to evacuate

Equipment and repair items

- **Tarps** and plastic sheeting
- **Rope**, twine, bungee cords
- **Duct tape** – lots of it
- **Hammer and nails** (and big washers) Roof nails, drywall nails, etc. hold better; the washers help the nails hold even more
- **Drill kit** (batteries, battery charger)
- **Chain saw**, lubricating oil
- **Hand saw, axe, crow bar, shovel**
- **Furring strips** (to keep the roof tarps in place better)
- An industrial strength **staple gun and staples** (for the soffit repairs)
- **Wooden stakes** to anchor anything that needs it – like ornamental trees, outside shed, etc. that the insurance company won't cover)

Home and yard

- **A generator.** If you've already got one have it serviced because it'll be real tough getting it serviced after the power goes out (Duh!)

Your emergency supplies kit

- Extension cords (heavy duty, 3 pin is best)
- Portable **A/C unit**, Portable **dehumidifier** or just an **electric fan**
- **Cooler** or ice chests (also good for storing documents in)
- **Paper plates**, plastic cups, flatware, etc. so you can throw away things you can't clean
- **Ziploc®**–type freezer bags for waterproof storage, aluminum foil for other storage
- **Disinfectant** Spray/liquid
- **Battery operated radio** or digital TV
- **Battery charger** for cell phones, etc. which run off your car battery
- **Flash lights** (one for each person is nice – and they're often given away as free gifts at sales events or sold cheaply at garage sales) and battery powered hurricane **lanterns** make a room feel more like home when there's no electricity and it's night time
- **Extra batteries** (including special ones for alarm clocks, hearing aids, smoke alarms, etc.)
- **Plastic bags** (with ties) for garbage, personal sanitation, etc.
- Large **bucket** (with lid) or a trash can with good lid. You might have to store stuff you'd normally flush away until it gets collected by waste management
- **Bucket**, mop, cleaning materials, old cloths, etc.
- **Household chlorine bleach** (unscented) to disinfect home surfaces and to disinfect water (or water purification tablets. Iodine also works)
- **A medicine dropper** to administer the correct number of drops of bleach (**or a tablespoon**) to possibly unsafe drinking and teeth-brushing water
- **Insect barrier spray** (or powder) to keep them out of your

home – they look for somewhere else to live if their homes are destroyed or after heavy rain.

- **Matches** to light the grill, **charcoal**, charcoal lighter fluid (or old newspaper) **propane, sterno, portable grill**

Personal items

- **"Work clothes"** like gloves, heavy footwear and dust masks and a hat

- **Wet weather clothes**

- **N-95 masks** (one per person) if there's mold in the air (or fiber glass)

- **Goggles** – also for when you're cleaning mold (and fiber glass)

- **First aid kit** (you might already have band aids, scissors, antiseptic cream, etc. so buy what you don't have rather than spending on a ready-assembled kit in its own presentation box. I know it's easier to buy a fully complete kit but it's cheaper not to.
   Sunscreen, lip balm, burn relief, aching muscle relief cream/wraps, joint supports, finger splint, bandages, gauze dressing, butterfly wound closures, tweezers, safety pins, eye pad, eye drops, petroleum jelly, cotton wool balls, antacid pills, anti-diarrhea pills. (Get another kit for the car)

- **Sanitizing gel** or towelettes so you can keep yourself and children as hygienic as possible when there's not enough water to wash with (a bout of diarrhea and no running water ain't fun)

- Liquid **soap**/bar soap, paper towels, deodorant

- **Personal hygiene items**, including toilet tissue (people forget to check how much they've got, apparently)

- **Contact lens** and similar cleaning fluids

- Extra supplies of **prescription medicines**, pain relievers, antacids, sprays, wraps or creams for aching muscles, etc.

- **Denture supplies**
- **Insect repellant**, itch relief cream
- **Drinking water** – officially, it's 1 gallon per person per day for 3 days. Personally I found it just wasn't enough. Have at least 2 gallons per person and, if you can, have 3 gallons. Apart from drinking like a camel when you work in the heat it's amazing how much water gets used (spilled) brushing teeth or just keeping clean (It'll be the Sagittarian in me)
- **Food** – at least 3 days supply of non-perishable food. If you have food in the freezer expect it to thaw by Day 3 (Day 2 if it's only half full – so fill it up with soda bottles of water – the less spoiled food you throw out the more money you save). You can still eat food once thawed as long as it gets cooked well; bacteria can start to multiply but enough cooking will kill it (but don't take chances – treat thawed food just like fresh food; it's got a limited life – and when in doubt, throw it out)

Get in "easy" food – food that doesn't need cooking, food that's tasty, food that's easy to chew and digest. Working hard in hot weather will ruin your appetite but you'll have to eat something, so make it something easy and tasty (canned meat, canned fruit, canned soups, canned beans, dried fruit, peanut butter, trail mix, crackers, cheese, energy bars, energy drinks, cookies, candy – that won't melt – instant coffee and tea bags)

Baby items
- **Food**, formula, etc.
- **Bottle, sterilizing kit**
- **Diapers**, wipes, talc, anti-rash cream
- **Clothes**, sleeping things
- **Toys**

People with special needs

If you are a person with special needs or if you have a relative or friend who has special needs **get advice** from your medical practitioner, social worker, or other professional and **register with your county Emergency Management Office.**
Special Care Centers might only open on an as-needed basis

- **Form a support group** or buddy system, if you haven't one already, so each knows to help the other. Make sure everyone in the group knows which medical or other professional should be contacted if you become incapacitated
- Make sure each "buddy" **can operate any special equipment**
- Make sure each "buddy" **can communicate with you or your relative properly** – and practice it
- Create an **appropriate emergency supplies** kit
- Know what **medications** might be needed and arrange for an appropriate supply – and put it in the Family File
- Have a list of specific **medical devices** which are used and know how to get replacements if needed
- Wear **medical alert tags** to help identify specific needs, quickly
- Pre-print important messages, if needed, to show to EMS staff

If you are responsible for someone who **resides in an ALF or nursing home**, check the following

- Know the **person at the facility you should be in contact with** (and their phone numbers) to ensure good communication in time of emergency
- **Know** the facility's **emergency management plan**

- **Confirm the plan** has been approved
- Confirm whether the **facility has stand-by generator power** and how they intend to deal with power failure if they do not have
- **How much of the facility** is serviced by the generator
- How much **emergency food, etc.** would the facility have on hand
- In what circumstances **would the facility be evacuated**
- **How will you be informed** if there is to be an evacuation
- What would **your expected role be** (if any) if the facility is to be evacuated
- **Where** might they be **evacuated to**
- **How** would you be able to **contact** them during and after evacuation
- **How** will they be **transported** to the new facility
- How will they be **transported back** when it is safe to do so
- How would your family member be released to you in order for them to be **evacuated with you**
- How would you **return them to the facility** afterwards

Caring for your pets

Plan for your pets! Make sure you get advice from your veterinarian or local humane society and also:-

- **Know if** your pet <u>will</u> be acceptable to a pet shelter (many only take dogs or cats). If not – locate a hotel/motel, boarding kennel, friend's house or even your veterinarian you can evacuate to where your pet will be welcome
- Have a recent photograph (in case they get lost or you evacuate to a shelter. **Unless you have certain things in place your pets can't go to a shelter.**
- Attach **ID tag** or (microchip ID), rabies tag, as appropriate, to your pet's collar
- Attach **your contact** details to the collar in case your pet gets lost
- Have an **up-to-date vaccination and other veterinarian records** to hand
- Get in extra **medications**
- Have a **suitable cage, crate or carrier** to keep them in. Let your pet get used to it, so they don't have to use it for the first time during an emergency – things will be difficult enough
- **Leash** and **muzzle**
- **If your pet will be accepted** at a shelter, have 3 days-worth of food (plus manual can opener), water, feeding/drinking bowls, medications, litter, paper towels, newspaper, disinfectant, plastic bags
- Take their **favorite toys**, blanket, etc.
- **Grooming supplies**
- **What if you can't take your pet with you when you evacuate?**

Most animals are natural survivors but natural disasters can disorientate them, fear can make a "friendly" animal into an aggressive one.

If in **extreme cases** you have to leave your pet behind help them out!

- **NEVER leave a pet outside on its own**
- Put them in a "safe" part of the house (inside, away from windows, etc.)
- Make sure they have **access to food and water** (including the toilet bowl)
- Put down newspapers to **protect your floors** as much as possible
- **Separate cats and dogs** even if they usually get on well
- **Put a notice up** where it can easily be seen saying there's an animal in the property, its name, the type of animal (Monty could be a python) and where the animal is.
- Include **your contact details** and those of your veterinarian
- **When you return** remember the animal might be afraid and aggressive
- When you **take your pet outside** keep them **on a leash** to prevent them from running away and getting lost or from foraging in the debris
- An animal that's considered dangerous is liable to be destroyed by the authorities

Evacuating safely and successfully

- **Agree, in advance, with your family what circumstances** will result in your evacuating

    E.g. Law Enforcement tells you to evacuate – it's mandatory

    Illness, injury, infirmity or other condition makes it a "better safe than sorry" decision

    You'd just rather ride out the storm in comfort and safety somewhere else

    To "save life and limb"

- **Decide where** you will, ideally, evacuate to.

    You might want a local place of refuge – you might live in a low-lying area but have friends a few miles away at a much higher elevation.

    Or a far-off place (even out of state). If you want to go to friends or family living elsewhere – agree it with them!

- If you decide to go to a hotel – **book as far ahead as possible.** Reserve by credit card, so you can cancel if your plans change

- Have a **second place** ready in case accident, illness or the storm path makes your first choice no longer possible

- Plan your **timing and route.**

- Plan an **alternative route** in case the road you want to use is "out of action" – it's become a parking lot because of other traffic, it's been flooded, whatever

- Remember that some roads can become **one-way streets** when emergency services declare a mandatory evacuation

- If your evacuation involves **buses, trains or airplanes** make sure the route will be available. If you book ahead use a credit card, so you can cancel if you change your plans

- Make sure each of your family members (or friends) has a **copy of the person's name, address, phone number(s), etc.** (for where you are going) just in case you get separated en route. I know it probably won't happen, but it might, so be prepared.

- Agree a **central contact person** (probably the person to whom you are evacuating) to act as a point of contact in case you do get separated or delayed

- Make a list of **everything you are taking** with you

- Make sure you all **pack everything** on your list

- **Decide whether** you will check your children's packing or do it together – helping each other helps kids feel more in control

- Decide what to do with your **pets** – see the chapter on pets

- Tell other family members, friends and neighbors about **your evacuation plan**, so they know that you'll be gone – and not to worry about you. And so they can contact you while you're gone – they'll know what shape your home is in better than you will!

  And **so they can plan as well** (so many people leave it to the last minute, so the evacuation is hurried and emotionally highly charged – and you lose your temper and the kids get frightened and it doesn't have to be like that!)

- Make a **"to do" list of actions before you evacuate** – what will you set the A/C to? Have you shut off the main water supply to the home? Which breakers will you set to "off"? That kind of thing. Seek advice from your Emergency Management Office

- If you are going to evacuate to a far distant place it is safe to shut off all power and water to the home

- **Public shelters**

  Remember – public shelters are **a place of "last resort"**. They are for people with no place else to go. They aren't designed for comfort or convenience.

They **won't have much in the way of facilities** and they probably won't take pets. So plan ahead and confirm whether your pet can go with you and what you should take

They'll be noisy, busy and crowded. **When the power fails they will not have light or air conditioning**

If you are or are responsible for **someone with special needs**, make sure you choose an appropriate shelter

- Go there expecting it to be noisy, busy and crowded. **Be considerate of others' issues.** Other people might be in panic, frustrated, fearful, tired.

- Be patient and cheerful – remember your **Family Treasure Chest of Strength**

- **Take your Emergency Supplies** – the shelter might not have food or water, etc. when you arrive

- **Take your own** bedding (and something to sit on)

- Take personal photo identification (and **unless the shelter you choose is pet-friendly**, the only animals allowed in will be documented service animals for people who have impaired hearing or vision)

- **Do NOT take firearms or alcohol.** In some areas you can get arrested

During the storm and after the storm

Remember that when winds reach 40mph, regular **police and sheriff deputy patrols will cease.**

Have a family meeting and help everyone feel ready

Remind everyone, especially your children, about how well you have all prepared. The wind and rain will be noisy but noise doesn't hurt. Remind them that you could all be in the storm's path for several hours, so plan your reading, games or other activities.

Be comfortable and stay safe
- **Stay away from windows**, even if they are covered
- **Collect what you each need** – games, books, radio, TV and things to keep you all comfortable
- Go to an **interior first floor room**
- **Close all interior doors**
- If the storm is severe use **additional protection** – go into a closet, cover yourselves with mattresses
- **Stay indoors** if there's a "calm", the eye of the storm will be followed by the trailing sector of more high wind
- **Keep everyone feeling positive** with conversation, stories, songs, prayer
- **Keep reminding** everyone that noise is to be expected
- **If the building begins to fail** decide whether to stay put and protect yourselves as much as you can or whether you should leave. Remember that most accidents are caused by people being hit by flying debris (especially glass) and by being caught in flood water
- **If you do decide to leave** follow your emergency evacuation plan

It's going to be a tough time after the storm! The better you prepared the less you will have to do.

Relax; pay attention to what your emotions, body and spirit tell you.

Give attention to your own well-being, to your family members' well-being and to also to your neighbors and friends.

Remember to use your Family Treasure Chest of Strength. Today really will be a day like no other.

Emergency management will have a great deal organized, even if it isn't all in place straight away. The State and national government will be getting in gear. Relief teams will be on their way. Insurance companies will be sending in their special disaster teams and many organizations like Red Cross will be very much "part of the solution"! They rely on you **not** to be part of the problems they will be working to solve.

Today is the day you will be grateful you prepared so well or regretful that you didn't. **Today is the day you meet yourself!**

If you evacuated to a safe place do what the authorities tell you to do – if it's safe to return you will be told; if not don't make things more difficult for disaster responders to do their jobs by getting in their way.

The chances are there will be no running water no working sewer system (your own septic system might be flooded out) no electricity, no telephone. Your home and your neighbors' homes might be anything from destroyed, to badly damaged, to livable.

Your street, your block, your neighborhood will look like a war zone.

Doing the wrong things can make it worse. Doing the right things will help to make it better.

Tell yourself and tell your family that this is just Day 1 and that everything will get better and better, so it's essential to stay positive.

First things first

- **Check you and your family members** are physically unhurt

During the storm and after the storm

- **Check the state of your home** – including above you in case there are low hanging objects. Check using a flashlight, not matches or candles
- **If you go outside** be careful where you stand, etc.
- **Look for** (and stay away from) any animals – ants, bees, snakes, vermin, loose domestic pets
- Secure the things you decide to (with **temporary repairs**) to make your home more safe and more livable. Do not exceed your capabilities; no one needs one more injured person to look after
- If you believe there are **damaged utility lines** (electricity, gas, etc.) leave the building
- Check to see if you have a **telephone service**. Call your out-of-area contact to report your status. Telephone service will be limited, so stay off the phone as much as possible so others, including emergency services, can use it
- **Help neighbors** who need it
- **Take pictures of damage** before and after any temporary repairs
- **Drive only if absolutely necessary** to leave roads clear for emergency services. If the lights are out at intersections remember to treat them as four-way stops
- **Assume public water is unsafe** to drink until authorities give the all-clear
- Remember to be extra vigilant about **personal hygiene**
- **Keep up to date about the current situation** by using your battery operated TV or radio
- **Take care of your pets** and remember they might be frightened and disoriented
- **Report power outages**, etc. as appropriate
- **Obey curfews**

Bust that stress

It's that *Cool Hand Luke* thing, again and it's important. You've got to get your mind right! Post-Disaster is when stress begins to take its toll on you and your loved ones. This is when you really do need to keep a clear head – **and it's not all that difficult.**

First-off accept that there are some things you can't do anything about – the weather, the outside utilities, the fact that everywhere looks trashed. Take a step back and accept that some things are going to be "as they are" and so you must focus on the things you can control – **begin with the end in mind**!

- **Gather everyone together.** Comfort each other, pray, ask for guidance from the Universe – do what feels right for you and your family. This is one of those occasions when you all *come together to be together*. It's calming and reminds everyone that you are all there for each other. And it's an occasion you can keep going back to so you keep reminding each other about it.

  Being stressed out and feeling out of control adds to the tiredness, the fear, the unhappiness. And they can result in the anger, fights and violence which so often get reported on as an almost natural result of living through a natural disaster.

  Many people never really – and I mean really – take a close look at themselves, their family members and their situation. Well if this is the first time – do it now. **Use your Family Treasure Chest of Strength** to give you all something positive to focus on, to lean on and to share with each other.

- **Agree to look out for each other.**

- **Agree a routine** with your family. It often happens that "routine" takes a back seat. That has several effects – things which should get done, don't get done, the list of jobs doesn't get shorter – so there are no little successes to enjoy, time gets wasted, stress builds up. So if you get a routine things feel better than they would

- **Include some R and R** in the routine. Watch TV or the radio at agreed times (it's too easy to sit glued to the TV getting the same sad news reports over and over, seeing the same pictures of devastation. So spend your non-work time doing something you enjoy

- **Agree to finish each job** as far as possible rather than doing a bit here and a bit there. Obviously some jobs will take a long time to complete but you can break them down into bite-size chunks and finish a "chunk" before moving on
- **Use a Check List** so you can check off jobs (or part jobs) so you all get a feeling of progress and you all get a sense of achievement
- **Keep Your Routine** as far as possible – get up at the same time, go to bed at the same time you normally would (within reason). If you normally read a little before you go to sleep, if you normally sit and talk with each other – keep doing it. The last thing to do is break those normal habits and replace them with stressful activities (like watching bad news reports or working until you drop (you'll get tired enough as it is). Even if you don't eat much – sit together at your regular meal times. Your body will thank you. Avoid too much "stress" food – if you don't normally eat lots of sugary foods don't start, your gut might not cope well with the change in diet
- **Keep to your schedule.** If you normally do certain things during the week – especially if they involve other people – keep doing them, as far as possible. You and they will feel better for it
- **Stay away from people who stress you out.** If you can help them to feel better, help them but if they just keep bringing you down you owe it to yourself and others who need you to avoid "doom-and-gloomers"
- **Keep checking in on yourself.** And give yourself little pats on the back. Ask yourself "What did I do this morning that was good? What could I do next time? How will that be better? And then when you do something a little different pat yourself on the back. And tell others so they can do a better job themselves, the next time

Either things get on top of you or you get on top of things – sometimes you'll succeed and sometimes you'll slip back a little. Stay on track, help others and ask others to help you. It will take time to get to the other side of the "disaster". It's a stressful time, so work to reduce the stress.

Cleaning up inside

It is essential to **get things clean and dry as soon as possible** to minimize the growth of mold and mildew as well as to maximize hygienic conditions.

Photographs and inventories will help when discussing things with your insurance loss adjuster. Keep receipts for everything you buy to help with clean-up and repair.

If the building is wet, dry it out as soon as possible (see the chapter on flooding).

Some of these notes assume, for example, you're returning after some time away and, e.g., your refrigerator is empty and the inside smells.

- **Clean** the outside of stoves and ovens with grease cutter and the insides with oven cleaner. Wash the door gasket as well as possible
- **Clean** the outside of other appliances the same way. Use detergent to clean the insides. Leave the doors open so they dry out well
- **Run your washing machine** with disinfectant on a hot water cycle
- **Stand books and papers on end to dry,** then press them and repeat until dry. Cornstarch will absorb dampness; brush off after a couple of hours
- **Photocopy important papers**, if you can in case the originals disintegrate
- **Wash from top to bottom** – start with ceilings and work down. Bleach will help sanitize, baking soda helps clean. White

vinegar helps get rid of odor

Keep checking toilet bowls in case of sewer back-up and clean accordingly

- **Leave electronic equipment to air-dry.** Never open the casing (e.g. of a TV since it can hold an electric charge). When you get electricity back, if the power light won't come on the item is probably still wet inside. If it comes on leave it on for 10 minutes, then unplug it, leave it for 30 minutes and turn it on again. This slowly gets electronic items completely dry inside. Never take risks with electricity and wet items

Cleaning up outside

•**Local authorities will remove items left at the curb as quickly as possible.** They will deal with rotting and dangerous items first, so stack items accordingly, to make it easier for them.

Never block roadways with piles of debris.

Typical collection priorities would be

1. Household garbage. Use regular garbage containers and heavy plastic bags
2. Yard waste. Keep it separate from garbage, have a communal pile for your street
3. Construction debris and household appliances (listen to the radio to learn when these things will be collected

Get debris out of your swimming pool as quickly as possible; it will leave rust spots that will never come off

Follow all safety rules when using heavy equipment like chain saws, when climbing ladders, etc. You will be tired, distracted, emotionally "down". Always stay focused on your own and others' safety. Stay alert for danger. Accidents are unforgiving!

Using a generator

If you get a portable generator **follow the rules** for using it.

Generators give off carbon monoxide. **Carbon monoxide is a killer** – one that has no color and no smell.

Keep generators away from enclosed spaces – not in a room, not in a garage, not close to a window, not between two houses if the distance between them is small. Generators must have free air around them.

Plug heavy duty extension cords into the generator and electrical items into the cord.

Do not overload the generator

Do not back-feed the generator into the house electric panel, it can cause a fire and it can electrocute utility workers

Generators get **very hot** do not touch them when they are on, do not stand anything on them, do not refill them until cool

Frequently **check fuel and oil** levels

Keep the generator dry

Hiring contractors

Out-of-area "contractors" will be down like a swarm of locusts. People who are now out of work will try to earn money (understandably) by offering themselves for hire as contractors.

Only hire suitably licensed contractors. Until you've lived through a natural disaster you won't believe how "good" people are at "selling you" on getting the job done – now.

You must decide whether you want a proper job done or not. It's your money, your home, your family's home. Permanent roof repairs, for example, should last for years, not weeks or months.

Being hit by a natural disaster wasn't your fault – being hit by an incompetent "contractor" will be your fault.

If the "contractor" doesn't have a suitable license will your insurance policy cover the cost?

If you don't have enough insurance cover **it might cost you more money** to make a quick decision to get a job done now – and then pay again to have it done properly. And it will definitely cost you more money if you pay a substantial deposit for materials and then have the contractor not show up again. These things can and do happen. **The less stressed you are the better your decisions** – that's all part of the forward planning and using your Family Treasure Chest of Strength.

If the "contractor" doesn't have proper insurance and he gets injured (or injures someone you care about) how will the claim be handled and will you be expected to pay? Apart from the heartache it could also cost you a lot of dollars.

And with the best will in the world, the contractor from 500 miles away will not come back to check on you or his workmanship. And he definitely won't be back if his workmanship was low quality.

Resist the temptation of a quick fix; keep the money in your community by hiring good, local contractors who will be there next month or next year.

Check your contractors' license details, check they have their own insurance, check they can do the work in the agreed timeframe, check your insurance company will accept the cost. Get proper quotes – your insurance company will need them. Only sign a contract for work that you are happy with – and your insurance company is happy with.

If you choose right you will have one less post-disaster issue to worry about. And you might just spend less money overall.

Protecting your boat

There are a number of obvious tasks that will not only protect your vessel but also save you money.

Before the storm
- If you use a **marina** or boat storage facility, check on rules, responsibilities, liabilities, etc.
- Check with the **boat's manufacturer** if you are unsure how to make everything secure
- Check **legal and other boat records** and keep them in a safe place – along with important phone numbers – insurance agent, harbormaster, Coast Guard, in case you need them afterwards
- Take **photographs** in case pre- and post-disaster condition has to be proven
- Make an **inventory** of what is on your boat and mark things with your name, address, etc. in case they get dispersed by a storm
- If your boat is **on a lift** secure it as high as possible to shorten the lift cables, so it won't blow about as much. And make sure the lift cables are in good condition
- Use **non-nylon rope**. Double all lines. Rig crossing spring lines fore and aft. Use one size above normal for one of your lines. Allow for rising water when you lash the boat
- Check all **pilings, cleats, etc.** that your boat will be tied to and repair as necessary
- Use **chafe protectors** as appropriate (tape, cloths, rubber hose)
- Install **fenders** to protect the boat as it moves in the storm
- Lash down or remove as much of the **movable things** on the boat as possible

- **Secure all openings** by locking – and sealing with duct tape
- Make sure the **bilge pump** is in good working order and the battery is fully charged
- If your boat is **on a trailer** use big ground anchors driven as deep as possible. Consider adding ballast (bilge water?) to increase the boat's weight
- Consider **other boats** upstream and modify your mooring if your boat could block another vessel's passage

After the storm

- **Check everything** to make sure you can board safely
- If your boat is full of water try to **clear the drain plug** without going on board
- Check for **snakes, crabs** or other harmful creatures
- Remove **hazardous items** like dead animals, rotting food
- Check for **electrical damage** like dangerous cables. Don't use lift motors if they might have been under water
- Report **theft**, etc. to law enforcement (storm damage to your insurance company)
- Check for **seaworthiness** before moving your boat
- Take **photographs** to compare with pre-damage pictures
- Make **temporary repairs** as necessary – don't compromise your insurance claim by doing permanent repairs before you are authorized to do so
- Inform appropriate authorities if your boat has **leaked pollutants** into the waterway
- Inform authorities if your boat has **sunk**
- Call your **insurance agent** then follow up with written details – exact location, structural condition, if it has to be removed where it will go to

Flooding is definitely worse

"Hide from wind. Run from water"
It's one of those basic rules you know; **water kills more people than wind.** And it's a sobering thought when it comes to natural disasters – about 9 out of 10 presidential disaster declarations involve flooding.

9 out of 10! That's a whole lotta floodin' goin' on. So it makes a whole lotta sense to prepare.

It's interesting to know that thousands upon thousands of people do not feel vulnerable to hurricanes or floods and yet **1000 people a year, on average, die because of flooding**. Then there are all the people who don't die, who don't even get injured, but whose lives and homes are totally disrupted by the disaster called "flood".

Flooding is a big worry, whether you live in a low-lying area or not. Hurricane Katrina's flood waters pushed 5 to 7 miles inland up through rivers and other waterways. Hurricane Charley was only "half a hurricane". It was a Cat 4 when it made landfall but because it was a tight-knit storm and traveled quickly it didn't build up a big storm surge, so it "only" generated about 7 feet. Flooding can be caused by lots of things – heavy rain and wind (obviously) high wind and high tide together, very heavy rain causing flash floods.

So let's look at flooding and how we can be ready.

There seem to be three general kinds of flooding:-

- Low-intensity flooding
- Storm surge flooding
- Flash flooding

I know they're all water and all cause the same basic problems but they each have their own unique calling cards.

Low intensity flooding is where, for example, water comes into your property because of a burst pipe, wind blows it under the doors – or up through the toilets and drains because of sewer back-up.

Storm surge is rather like a tsunami – a wall of water coming at you, destroying everything in its path.

Hurricane Katrina was a Cat 3 when it made landfall (it had been a Cat 5 out in The Gulf) and it delivered up to 28 feet of storm surge that went 5 to 7 miles inland. Hurricane Ike was 'only' a Cat 2 when it made landfall – but the storm surge was 25 feet. **And 34 people are still missing.**

As they say – run from water!

Flash flooding, often caused by heavy rain (or rapid snow melt if you live up north) and can vary from a few inches of fast moving water to a surge wall of up to 20 feet.

Even if you just get a couple of feet of flash flood you can expect a lot of fast-moving debris (which hurts). 6 inches of flash flood can knock you (or your child) off your feet. 2 feet of flash flood can wash away your car. That's why a lot of people die – they get knocked off their feet or the vehicle they are in gets washed off the road.

Something a lot of people never think about is how heavy water actually is. Flood water doesn't just wash away foundations it can actually break the walls of a building.

Unless the water destroys a building because of its force or weight it will get everywhere. It will seep through drywall. Within two days, mold starts to grow.

Water carries everything with it – sewer back-up carries the obvious, overflowing rivers, sheet flow, etc. carry sand, silt, mud, fish, it's all in the flood water. To say nothing of ants, snakes, road kill – and they all finish up where the water leaves it. Floods can be horrible events!

So **floods bring their own unique issues**. It's just as important to prepare for them as it is for wind and there's one big difference – water does more damage. I know my home is rated to withstand winds of more than 130 mph, so a Cat 1 hurricane shouldn't disrupt my home life too much.

But an extra few inches of water will!

High wind hurls things at the outside of your home; high water brings it inside – one grain of sand and one morsel of rotting organic matter, one snake at a time! Someone else's roof shingles lying in your yard won't smell, make your family ill or bite you; what the water brings into your home will!

That's one of the big differences – so prepare as well as possible!

General before the flood actions

Prepare with your family, just like for a hurricane

- Check your **insurance policy**! Flood insurance, per se, requires a separate policy. BUT you might be able to buy extra cover through your home owner policy just to cover sewer back-up. You can check for nothing!

- If you buy a **new policy** remember it has to be in force for at least 30 days before it's active

- Check to see if you live in a **designated special flood hazard area**, SFHA, (call your county EMO)

- Find out what **the flood history** is for where you live. You might not be in an SFHA but your street or block might flood and that will block your evacuation route

- **Stockpile a home defense kit** – heavy plastic sheeting (the sort you can use to seal damaged or missing soffits), lumber, nails, a shovel, bags you can fill with earth or sand to act as a temporary water barrier

- Check out how to stack **sandbags** so they provide maximum protection for your particular home or office situation

- Install **check valves** in sewer traps to prevent back-up. Or, a cheaper but not so effective way, is to get large bungs or stoppers to plug tub and shower drains

- If you consider evacuating, definitely **know more than one route** out – flash flooding can block your path better than windblown debris can

- Get **up-to-date maps** – local maps are often available from your local Realtor®

Just before-the-flood actions

- **Stay in touch** with those you need to and listen to the radio/TV for the latest info about your area
- Know where your family members are and do what you all agreed you would do about getting together or making your own way
- **Review** your "Family Plan"
- Get your **emergency supplies** organized
- If told to evacuate – leave ASAP (see evacuation plan below)
- **If you are staying** – clean the bath tub, sinks, etc. and fill them with usable water. Floods will contaminate the regular water supply, so get some in
- **Raise everything** you can as high as possible. Put valuable possessions on the plant shelves, for example. You can even stand wooden furniture on cement blocks (or even cans of food) to protect it from a few inches of flood water – not all flooding is disastrous but a few inches can still ruin what you own
- **Protect** the places where water can easily get in – use the plastic sheets, sand bags, etc.

Just after-the-flood actions

- If you left the area – only **return when authorities say** it is safe to do so
- **Inspect** foundations and stem walls for damage
- **Stay out** of buildings if they are still flooded
- If you go through **standing water** and when you first re-enter

your home wear rubber knee-boots (what I call Wellington boots, named for the Duke of Wellington – of Waterloo fame) if there are ants, snakes or whatever you should be safer from attack with the right footwear. And use a stick, or similar, to poke through debris in your home. Most snake bites are to people's hands and forearms!

- Call your insurance agent **and agree what level of repairs you can do**

- **Watch out for damaged ceilings or anything similar** that could fall on you – most people only look "down' when searching and investigating – remember to look "up" as well! (I still have a scar on my forehead because I was walking carefully through a damaged house and crashed straight into a fallen beam – also hurts)

- **Look for** fire and health hazards – **damaged gas lines, loose or exposed electrical cables.** "Buzzing" sounds which might be a shorted out cable, submerged electrical panel or outlet. "Hissing" sounds might indicate a broken gas line

If you planned your evacuation you will have turned off your electric, gas and water but be careful, anyway – especially if you are at a different property, like a neighbor's house

If you do suspect electrical or gas leaks, **leave the property and contact a licensed professional for advice. Never go through water to turn off an electrical circuit (Duh!)**

- **Look out for dangerous materials** which might have been washed in with the flood water, e.g. flammable or explosive materials – is it possible any camping stove or firearm materials could be lying around? You know what was in your home and what might have been in your neighbors' so be careful – and remind your children to be careful!

- When appropriate **check to see if your sewer or septic system is possibly damaged** – do not use the toilets – and call a licensed professional. If your drain field is obviously under water it's very likely your septic tank is full of flood water (and whatever flowed in with it), so get professional help

- **If you have a basement** and it's flooded it should be drained slowly (about one-third of the water a day) to avoid structural damage
- If you have a **contaminated swimming pool** – drain that slowly, as well, to minimize the risk of it "popping" out. The pool skin is under pressure from the water in it and the earth around it – remove all the pressure from inside the pool too quickly by draining it and you could damage the pool beyond repair

Drinking water

- **Assume all water is unsafe** to drink until treated – unless your water authority tells you it's safe
- **Conserve water as much as possible** – it'll be in short supply
- **If your well** was covered by flood water, disinfect it, then have it tested before you use the water

After-the-flood clean-up

Flood clean-up requires a lot more thought, effort and care than wind damage clean-up. It really does require many special precautions.

Take lots of photographs to prove what was damaged – the loss adjuster won't be there for a long time after you've done your flood clean-up

Sanitation and hygiene

Let's start with the obvious – **boil** or otherwise disinfect **all water you use**. (Rolling boil for two minutes, use sterilizing tablets according to the label)

Wash hands before touching food, after using the bathroom or touching anything unsanitary (like hauling debris to the curb). Use antibiotic creams and sterilizing gels, especially if you've got a cut or graze.

Keep an extra watch on children – where they play and what they play with!

Dealing with mold

Mold starts to grow after a couple of days. Mold needs damp to grow (over 60% humidity in the atmosphere, let alone soaking wet walls and carpets). Molds can cause disease and cause allergic reactions. Mold also continues to damage property after a flood has subsided.

- **Get rid of flood water** as soon as you can (unless it's got oil floating on it – you must remove the oil first otherwise it will coat your walls and floors. Do not discharge oil into the outside as it can contaminate well water
- **Remove damaged property** (like carpets)
- **If things have been soaked by flood waters and sewage** you've probably got 48 hours to clean, dry and treat them before you'll have to throw them away
- **Ventilate and dry** as well as you can – fans, dehumidifiers, etc.
- **Get professional help** to get rid of mold
- **Always wear rubber boots and gloves** when working with mold, debris and cleaning materials. **Wear a face mask** rated an N-95 respirator and goggles without vent holes. Mold will get through regular dust masks and kerchiefs.
- **Clean walls and floors with soap and water** then disinfect with a solution of 1 cup of bleach to 5 gallons of water

Take extra care when cleaning anywhere that food will be prepared and where there are children

- **Be careful about mixing household chemicals;** they can generate toxic fumes and can result in injury or death – read the labels, don't guess. If in doubt – don't mix.
- **Disinfect A/C and heating ducts** if they've been in contact with flood water

- **Wash all linens and clothing** or have them professionally laundered/dry cleaned
- **If things cannot be laundered or dry-cleaned** – e.g. mattresses, upholstered furniture – they should be air dried outside (if good weather) and thoroughly sprayed with a disinfectant (or throw out)
- **If you <u>can</u> save your carpets** have them steam cleaned
- **Replace insulation** if it got wet
- **Replace you're A/C and other air filters**
- **Remember that your clean-up will create** a huge amount of garbage. **Garbage invites vermin and insects** (their 'homes' were also destroyed) looking for food since their own food source probably got destroyed. Use watertight and pest-resistant containers to store the garbage ready for collection. Your local authority will keep you informed about collection days
- **Keep piles of garbage** away from wells
- **Set rodent traps** if you need to
- **Keep emptying things that hold standing water** – they're a breeding ground for mosquitoes
- **Wash and <u>disinfect</u>** food containers – or throw them away
- **Wash and <u>disinfect</u> cans of food** (immerse for 5 minutes in a bleach solution – 2 tablespoons of bleach per gallon of water) unless the cans are damaged, rusted, swollen or you can't identify what's inside
- **Throw away food containers with screw tops or pressed tops** (soda and beer bottles) – they cannot be disinfected properly
- **Disinfect plates, cups, dishes and flatware** by immersing in bleach solution (2 tablespoons/gallon of water)
- **Boil real silverware** for 2 minutes in clean water (bleach ruins silver)

Afterword

I hope you enjoyed the story and I hope, as you went through the lists of things to do and things to think about, you got the same feeling that I did – that you know you and your family will be safer, stronger and "ready". I also hope you say the same about your home, even though you'll mean it in a different way.

Any natural disaster is traumatic. Some are totally devastating and no matter how much anyone prepares no ordinary building can withstand strong Category 5 winds or a tsunami of flood water. If that's what happens to you then the chapter on how best to evacuate is probably all you'll really get from the list of practical things to do. But if, like most people, your home and community survive with damage then I truly hope this book did its job for you, for your family and for your community.

Thank you!

Tony Gillen
P.O Box 511062
Punta Gorda
Fl 33951

www.UpsideOfHurricanes.com

Appendix

Useful web sites

There are many government and non-government Web sites where you can find detailed as well as general information which might be just what you are looking for. Here's a list.
(Muchos Web Sites tienen versiones en español)

Government sites

Always begin with your own state and county government site. It will have information which is directly relevant to you and where you live. It will also have useful phone numbers and addresses. Your local TV, radio and newspaper Web sites will also have a huge amount of useful and local information.

Before hiring a contractor, check out your state licensing authority (if you don't know it you can search under those three words)

Be Ready Campaign	www.ready.gov
Federal Emergency Management Agency	www.fema.gov
Department of Homeland Security	www.dhs.gov
Dept of Health and Human Services	www.hhs.gov/disasters
National Oceanic & Atmospheric Administration	www.noaa.gov
National Weather Service	www.nws.noaa.gov
Centers For Disease Control and Prevention	www.cdc.gov
Citizen Corps	www.citizencorps.gov
Outside Air Quality Warnings	www.airnow.gov
Small Business Administration	www.sba.gov

Non-Government sites

American Red Cross	www.redcross.org
Salvation Army	www.salvationarmy.org
Institute for Business and Home Safety	www.ibhs.org

Breinigsville, PA USA
19 October 2009
226052BV00004B/2/P